# before the
# thunder
# rolls

## devotions for
## NASCAR fans

# before the
# thunder
# rolls

## devotions for
## NASCAR fans

## Dale  Beaver

Forewords by Jimmie Johnson
and Ryan Newman

VALLEY FORGE, PA

BEFORE THE THUNDER ROLLS: Devotions for NASCAR Fans
© 2007 by Judson Press, Valley Forge, PA 19482-0851
All rights reserved.

Library of Congress Cataloging-in-Publication Data
Beaver, Dale. Before the thunder rolls : devotions for NASCAR fans / Dale Beaver ; forewords by Jimmy Johnson and Ryan Newman. —1st. ed. p. cm.
ISBN 978-0-8170-1521-3 (pbk. : alk. paper) 1. Stock car racing—United States. 2. Automobile racing fans—Prayers and devotions. 3. NASCAR (Association) I. Title. GV1029.9.S74B43 2007
796.720973—dc22                                    2007035088
Printed on recycled paper in the U.S.A.
First Printing, 2007.

Author photo by Todd Burnett, vpstudiodesigns.com.
Front cover: ©Action Sports Photography, Inc.

To Andree, my wife,
for saying yes to
my marriage proposal
the same night she
taught me to ice skate;

to Adam for introducing
me to fatherhood;

to Andrew for usually
making me smile;

to Darren Michael for reminding
me that Candyland is the
best game ever;

and to David Henry for
giving me glances from
blue eyes that stir my soul.

And to Mom and Dad,
Terri and Darren Scott—
it all started with you,
ESPN, and the television
in the "Big Room."

# contents

# foreword

I started racing motorcycles when I was five, and we treated the trips to the track as a family event. My mom, dad, and brothers were all involved. Those years provided an awesome context in which to grow up. Even now, I am blessed to be able to enjoy my true passions in life on a daily basis—my wife, Chandra, and racing.

Like any sport, racing has its ups and downs. We celebrate the victories and press on through the disappointments. These highs and lows can fluctuate from one weekend to the next—certainly from one season to the next. The need for a spirit of determination and preparation is as crucial to racing as it is in all of life.

A lot of times fans miss out on just how much work has gone into a driver's career. You have to make it a labor of love, and even when you do, it's still very difficult climbing through the ranks. The hard work doesn't stop when you arrive at the NASCAR Sprint Cup Series. The competition is fierce. The drive to produce winning results is relentless. I realize that from the stands it may be difficult to see the effort involved. Let me assure you that a tremendous amount of preparation has taken place to get the teams and their equipment race ready.

In this book, my friend Dale Beaver will help you appreciate that preparation and parallel it to your own life.

Chandra and I had the pleasure of spending time with Dale during his time as chaplain in the NASCAR community. His Sunday morning sermons with Motor Racing Outreach always started our weeks on the right foot. Dale's friendship is invaluable and his ministry uplifted our lives. You'll discover as you read that he has done his homework on our sport from the inside out.

Whether you are a race fan or just someone interested in the landscape of what has become the fastest-growing spectator sport in America, you will be enlightened and often challenged by what you find in this book. Dale writes with a passion for the people he served, and you will see firsthand how he led the racing community on our spiritual journey. It is our hope that you will discover the similarities between race preparations and the preparations we all need to make in life. Chandra and I join Dale in inviting you to trust God in your daily life before the thunder rolls.

God's best to you,
Jimmie Johnson
Car #48

# foreword

In the hectic world of auto racing, there is very little time to attend church ceremonies on Sundays. When I began driving in the NASCAR Sprint Cup Series, Motor Racing Outreach was there to offer a time of prayer and reflection. MRO, as we call it, is a small community of people that travel within the NASCAR circuit to offer support, faith, and guidance for drivers, families, and crewmembers.

Dale Beaver was part of MRO as the Cup series chaplain. In his Sunday chapel services he related what I do in my everyday life to stories in the Bible. At long last I was able to focus on and understand many of the messages taught in Scripture. I inevitably left Dale's chapel service with a new understanding of the Bible and a practical life lesson. It was in those brief 20-minute sermons on Sunday mornings that I really began to understand God.

Dale was not only a chaplain, but he became a friend. In 2003 I proposed to my girlfriend, Krissie. She had attended many chapel services with me, and we both agreed wholeheartedly that we wanted Dale to perform the wedding ceremony. He sat with us on several premarital counseling sessions, discussing the challenges in marriage and teaching us how to communicate on a different level with God in our lives. Many of those principles you will find in this book as well. It is evident in being around Dale and his wife, Andree, that they are an example of true faith, love, and companionship.

Now the wisdom and insight that Dale has offered to me and others in the NASCAR community are available to you. Many of the stories that encouraged and challenged me have become chapters in this book. One of them (Chapter 3) has provided a constant reminder to me of how God touches our everyday lives. Dale was discussing life's choices and referenced a "surface plate"— the common template we use in the race shop to build our cars so we have accurate measurements at the race track. Life has a surface plate as well, Dale taught us. God has given us this surface plate—his Word. As we go through life, we can make choices based on truth, and we can change the balance.

Dale is an inspirational personality. Krissie and I are just two of the people he has touched and brought closer to God! He has been a friend, a mentor, and a confidante to everyone he meets. He has poured himself into the stories and reflections in this book. Enjoy these devotions, but leave with a greater understanding of the God who makes Dale, and all of us, the people we are.

God Bless,
Ryan Newman
Car #12

# acknowledgments

I love to tell stories, especially when I have experienced the subject matter. People have affirmed me in that vocation, and I hope that when you finish reading this book, you will feel the same way. My desire for you is that as you read this book you will find yourself more knowledgeable about NASCAR racing and, most particularly, how it illustrates certain aspects of your spiritual life. With that understanding, my prayer is that you never look at racing in the same way again, but will be reminded of all the ways God is speaking to you through it.

Having said this, I must thank Rebecca Irwin-Diehl and Judson Press for spurring me on to write this collection of thoughts. My desire to do so needed encouragement. Special thanks to Eric Quinn, the finest motor sports athletic trainer in the business, for helping me with certain athletic facts, and to John Jeppeson for giving me insights into the technical background of the sport that I had disregarded or simply missed over the years.

My heartfelt appreciation goes to pastor and author Dr. David Haney. You remain my friend and mentor in all things communicatively creative. I aspire to be like you as a man of God at work in the world. To Mark Thelen, who has been like Christ to me since 1989 and remains my closest friend. (I need Braves tickets!)

To Jim Cote, Max Helton, and Ron Pegram, three guys who saw something in me that God could use in the sport of auto racing. I hope you don't regret it!

To my dearest ones, Andree and the Beaver boys. I knew at a very early age that I wanted to be married and have a family. The five of you have exceeded my wildest dreams. I would be lost without you.

To Christian Fellowship Church in Evansville, Indiana, for making me feel at home in such a short time.

And to Jesus. Like Paul—perhaps the only way I am like him—I will always live in the tension of longing to be with you while loving the life you've placed me in here.

# introduction

The mere pursuit of health always leads to something unhealthy. Physical nature must not be made the direct object of obedience; it must be enjoyed, not worshipped.

G. K. Chesterton

My mission is to ruin your perspective on the sport of stock car racing. There you have it. But before you put down this book, hear me out. I believe that most people need their perspectives on their favorite sports ruined—at least a little. If you are reading this as an American, let's confess together that we love our sports, at times, more than we should. Don't believe me? How much money did you invest in your favorite sport this year—travel, tickets, equipment, apparel? How does that figure compare with what you gave away?

I'm not saying that you should abandon being a "fan" of racing. I'm just saying that maybe you should be a little less fanatical. My desire is that you read this book for a fresh perspective, a spiritual one whereby you look at the sport differently. I hope that as you finish the last page, you will not be able to witness a race, in person or on television, without remembering the biblical principles attached to those images and situations. To follow Chesterton's wisdom, my prayer for you is that you will always seek the Creator above all of creation—even recreation. Relax. Enjoy. But reserve your offering of worship—your daily sacrifice of praise and service—for the One from whom all blessings flow.

Now let's start preparing for the race of life by learning how racers prepare for their weekends. You will be amazed at how the mental, physical, and spiritual aspects of driver and machine mold together. This has to happen before the thunder rolls.

# part 1

## IT STARTS IN THE SHOP

Racing teams love to run well "off the truck." If they have tested the car well, taken great notes, and translated that into value while in the shop, they will have a faster race car during the first practice session—and that will make for a much easier day. The more preparation completed at home, the better a team performs, mentally and physically, at the track.

Jesus told his followers after he had risen, "Do not leave Jerusalem until the Father sends you what he promised" (Acts 1:4). The place each of us calls home should be a haven for the earliest work of God in our lives. Home is where we lay the foundation for growing in our devotion to the Lord. It is never too early to start the process of knowing God. Do so with those you love—at home—in the shop.

# 1

## WE DON'T JUST SHOW UP

> Therefore, since we are surrounded by such a huge crowd of witnesses to the life of faith, let us strip off every weight that slows us down, especially the sin that so easily hinders our progress. And let us run with endurance the race that God has set before us. We do this by keeping our eyes on Jesus, on whom our faith depends from start to finish. He was willing to die a shameful death on the cross because of the joy he knew would be his afterward. Now he is seated in the place of highest honor beside God's throne in heaven. Think about all he endured when sinful people did such terrible things to him, so that you don't become weary and give up.
>
> Hebrews 12:1-3

Race fans know that their favorite sport is not taken seriously by many supporters of the "ball" sports. Drivers and crewmen are often disregarded as athletes. I used to buy into and promote that misunderstanding myself. Not until my father actually took me to my first race, the 1991 Daytona 500, did I get a feel for the intense demands of this sport.

It was an unusually cold day as I watched from my seat in row 28 of Weatherly Tower. The wind was a relentless lash, but it didn't seem to bother the sea of humanity down on the infield making last-minute preparations for the race. I turned to the gentleman sitting next to me and asked if he knew how long it took to get everything ready. "Let's see," he said, "the last race ended the week before Thanksgiving of last year, so . . . since the day after Thanksgiving. They don't just show up here, ya know!" I didn't know. I was stunned.

Every year the NASCAR Sprint Cup Series winds down with the final race taking place just one week before the holiday. Many of the teams return from that race and immediately start working on their cars for February's Daytona 500. It is called the "off-season"—that period of time between the final race and the start of next season—but no one is really "off." The teams work incessantly to prepare for Daytona. Unlike the Super Bowl, the biggest event of the racing calendar is the first. Every team wants to make the most of this starting opportunity. Even a last-place finish at Daytona ensures as much prize money as a win at other events—and nearly as much prestige.

It's a big deal. The race teams don't just show up. They prepare by working long hours covering the tiniest strategic details. Adequate preparation is measured by fractions of seconds, and it's those fractions that can separate a top-ten car from a last-place car. From engines to suspensions, gauges to nuts and bolts, every resource is scrutinized to make a race car the best it can be. It can often be a radical endeavor. I once asked Ward Burton if his practice session was going well. "Terrible!" he shot back. "We're changing everything but the paint on this car."

Keep in mind that our daily activity isn't part of some dress rehearsal for another existence. The writer to the Hebrews tells us that life is like a race, and like the Daytona 500, it's a race of endurance as much as speed. God has shown us how we are supposed to run—the course is set before us. Through the example of Jesus and his sacrificial death on the cross for us, our Creator has spared no expense to prepare us for this life and the next. Others have run this race as well, and it is this "crowd of witnesses" who cry out to us from Scripture to keep going, to keep pressing on.

Just like you, those in the biblical hall of fame lost faith at times and wrestled with God's plan for their lives. These heroes and heroines made the same mistakes we make, and many of them went further up the rebellion scale than most of us have. The thing all of them have in common that I hope you will find is true of you as well is the commitment to press on in faith and keep believing. Unlike me that day at Daytona, and countless other fans who have no idea what it is like to endure such a grueling challenge, the spectators who cheer us from a biblical perspective (Hebrews 12:1) know what it is like to thrive and to fall in the race of life. They have been where we are—and they finished well.

## PIT NOTE

Darrell Waltrip started the Daytona 500 *seventeen* times before he won the race. His persistence paid off. He never gave up. Ask Holy Spirit Lord to remind you daily that life with God is not a sprint. It's a walk—together.

# 2

## TUBULAR STEEL AND MARKET APPEAL

> But the LORD said to Samuel, "Don't judge by his appearance or height, for I have rejected him. The LORD doesn't make decisions the way you do! People judge by outward appearance, but the LORD looks at a person's thoughts and intentions."
>
> 1 Samuel 16:7

> "You have patiently suffered for me without quitting. But I have this complaint against you. You don't love me or each other as you did at first! Look how far you have fallen from your first love! Turn back to me again and work as you did at first."
>
> Revelation 2:3-5

NASCAR Sprint Cup Series race shops are pristine works of art. Most people who have never seen these beautiful structures would assume a sight completely different. Gone are the days when engines were pulled by hoists supported by shade tree branches. Greasy gravel floors are a thing of the past. And garages no longer double as tobacco barns. With a visit to the Charlotte, North

Carolina, fans can view their favorite teams at home in a theater-like environment.

Such sites are testimonies to the corporate-driven success and persona that great marketing can produce. Sitting with driver Bobby Labonte and his crew chief at the time, Jimmy Makar, I was schooled on the professional shift that comes at this level: "Before you get to Cup, it's easy to focus on the racing aspect of your game. When you get to this level, it's called a 'show'; every race is like being in a TV commercial. That's really difficult to get used to. You work hard to get to this place, and truthfully everyone wants to be here, but it is so different from what you experienced in the past."

The teams need the corporate image to fuel the growth and success of the sport. It is that image, however, that can get in the way of racing in its purest form. The passion that drives the competitive spirit often has to spin on a dime and represent the products and services of corporate America. It is easy to see how some of the veteran drivers and crew members could eventually lose heart. Professional athletes often lose their own identities within the machine of marketing—and racers are not immune. A great building with all the finest technology and flash that money can buy cannot generate the team chemistry needed to succeed. Go looking off the beaten path, and that is usually where you will find the men and women who are having the most fun racing. Rewarded with all that they have, Cup racers will tell you that those days in off-the-beaten-path places—often dirt tracks— were full of character development. There they determined who they were and what they wanted to do with their lives.

As a child, I was struck by the reality of who God is and how God relates to us. The Lord is not impressed with your external giftedness. You may not be the strongest or the fastest or the best-looking. That is not the stuff that counts with Christ. He judges the intentions of your heart. He is the author of judging persons not by outward appearances but by the hearts. Thankfully, God does not draw us to himself based on our market appeal!

In the first book written by the prophet Samuel, we see that Israel was not satisfied with having the Creator of the universe as their king. They wanted a leader like the other nations—impressive and strong—but looks can be misleading. Though a person may appear to be loaded with credentials on the outside, he or she may lack the most important characteristic—the heart of a servant under the authority of God. That is the trait in us that God values most.

What about you? Feeling swayed by the draw of image and prestige? Success is really a greater danger than failure if you forget the reasons why you were put here to begin with. In the last book of the Bible, the apostle John records Jesus' words to an affluent church in a place called Ephesus. Christ admonishes the congregation of his followers there to remember him first in all they do (Revelation 2:1-7). John would write nothing different to us today.

## PIT NOTE

When was the first time you recognized God's presence at work in your life? Where were you? What was the circumstance? Was that the start of a growing faith, or did the moment simply pass? How are you different now since then?

# 3

## THE SURFACE PLATE

All Scripture is inspired by God and is useful to teach us what is true and to make us realize what is wrong in our lives. It straightens us out and teaches us to do what is right. It is God's way of preparing us in every way, fully equipped for every good thing God wants us to do.

2 Timothy 3:16-17

If the Bible is nothing more than fables and fairy tales, then the Ten Commandments are nothing more than suggestions. As bad as the world is, can you imagine how it would be if everyone thought God's law was optional?

Grandpa Beaver

After relocating to Charlotte, North Carolina, the first race shop I visited was the Ford powerhouse of Robert Yates. The engines produced by this team are legendary. Robert and his son, Doug, are still revered in the sport as pioneers of horsepower, and I felt more than privileged to receive a personal tour of the facility. Upon arrival I made two immediate observations—neither of which involved an actual race car. First, it was so clean one could eat off the floor, and second, there was a large, slightly raised rectangle in the middle of the floor. The rectangle, brilliantly finished with the Robert Yates Racing logo embedded near one end, was the focal point of the shop.

"Doug, what is that?" I asked.

He grinned, knowing that I was very new at this. "That is a very critical piece of equipment," he replied.

*Equipment,* I thought, *a piece of the floor?*

"That's the surface plate, a perfectly level platform we use to set up the chassis of a race car. Every car we take to the track gets its reference points from that plate."

"Why?" I asked.

Doug answered me as simply as he could. "Because we know that a measurement from that surface is true. There will be no variance from the front of the car to the back. We spent a lot of money for that assurance. Chassis setups need that kind of precision."

"So a surface plate is the racer's Bible, if you will—your standard of truth?" I chimed in.

"You could say that. It really fits," he observed.

From the time of that first visit with Doug Yates, I never visited any other race facility where I didn't pause and reflect for a moment by their respective surface plate. Some were equally as ornate, but some were simply plain but polished metal. Like our Bibles, it is the function of the surface plate that makes it valuable, not the form.

I remember Jeff Gordon asking me once if I had a particular translation of the Scriptures that he could have. He had given his copy to a friend and wanted to replace it. I replied, "Sure! You a hardback or softcover man?"

He rolled his eyes at me.

"No, really," I returned. "It makes a difference to me."

He came back immediately. "Beav', as long as I can read the words, that's all that matters to me."

That was a great lesson for me. Ouch! I had become a connoisseur of the packaging. Jeff simply wanted the substance therein.

How much then is the standard of truth worth? Race teams are committed to paying dearly for it. Throughout history, many people have paid dearly to have the Word of God as well. Some have offered up their lives so that the most common men and women in the most remote places in the world could possess the light of the written gospel. More than likely you can take a short drive in your community and find many copies of God's Word in various sorts of translations and presentations. The availability of this assortment can potentially blunt the gratitude we should convey for the privilege of owning a copy of the Bible.

Regardless of the packaging, the bottom line is that you *can* possess the written revelation, the wisdom of God, for your review every day. Without the consistent foundation of truth that we find in the Bible, our lives are riding on a surface that twists and turns with the philosophical flavor of the day. Without a scriptural surface plate, you would determine your own morality, and so would I. This sounds good until either of us is wounded by what we justify as right or wrong. We need God for an unchanging standard, not our situational morality.

Juris doctor and author Arthur Allen Leff expressed our need for divine law in a well-written piece for the *Duke Law Journal*.

[Without absolute morality] it looks as if we are all we have. Given what we know about ourselves and each other, this is an extraordinarily unappetizing prospect; looking around the world, it appears that if all men are brothers, the ruling model is Cain and Abel. Neither reason, nor love, nor even terror seems to have worked to make us "good," and worse than that, there is no reason why anything should....God help us.*

Indeed God has! Without the truth of Scripture, we are like race cars built on shifting sand. It need not be so. We have the surface plate for our lives between the covers of our Bibles. Be it softcover or hardcover, King James or a modern paraphrase, take your measurements from the wisdom of God's Word.

## PIT NOTE

Why do you read God's Word? Some read to gain an upper hand on others. They read so they will be right. Others read to try and find errors within. They hope to discredit God. Both of these motives are off base. Read your Bible to discover the truth about God and the truth about yourself. You will be amazed by what you learn.

*Arthur Allen Leff, "Unspeakable Ethics, Unnatural Law," *Duke Law Journal* December 1979, 1249.

# 4

## THE DYNO ROOM

> Search me, O God, and know my heart; test me and know my thoughts. Point out anything in me that offends you, and lead me along the path of everlasting life.
>
> Psalm 139:23-24

On a table in my office stands a 1:4 scale Hendrick Motorsports replica race motor. A limited number of these were made for the friends of the late Randy Dorton. Randy died along with several of his coworkers when a team plane, 501RH, crashed into Bull Mountain near Stuart, Virginia. The cohorts were on their way to the fall 2004 Martinsville race. I was at the track as usual and will never forget the grief of that foggy morning. I wasn't ready to say good-bye to Randy. I don't know anybody who was.

Randy was described by his fellow competitors as a "mechanical magician," and his engines won numerous races and not a few championships in the NASCAR Sprint Cup Series. Sportswriter John Jeppesen knew Randy and marveled at his abilities as well. While covering a TV spot for a brand of motor oil, John tried to pin Randy down on how he made such great horsepower for his teams. Was it the motor oil? "Peanut butter," was all Randy would say.

He wasn't about to divulge trade secrets. Whatever came from Randy's touch, it was nothing short of phenomenal and deeply coveted.

Randy hosted my first look inside a premier racing engine program. As I walked with him that day, I was amazed at the many intricate parts and manipulations of those parts—and I still do not understand how they all come together to make something called "horsepower." I think Randy was so free in walking me around because he knew that I wouldn't know a trade secret if I saw one. There was one place, however, that he would not let me enter. He didn't call it a secret place, but I found out later that it was—the place where race teams test their power plants, the "dyno (short for dynamometer) room."

In the dyno room, race engines are tested at high rpm to determine their output and dependability. In this room, critical questions find answers: "How hard can I run this thing?" and "How will fuel economy be affected at these speeds?" And for some reason, this highly classified room of raw horsepower was off-limits to me on that particular day—and maybe any other day.

In the dyno room, engineers listen to a language spoken by those controlled explosions that only their trained ears can understand. What these engineers hear determines the maximum potential for horsepower and efficiency on the racetrack. Nothing is more important than listening to what those engines say under the severe strain of high rpm—a test to learn what each device can take.

Maybe you are under the strain of losing a dear friend, a spouse, or a career. Perhaps you are stuck in limbo somewhere, losing hope that God has a purpose for your life. You may feel as if your life is in God's dyno room. The pain of living in a fallen world forces us to allow our Creator to push us to the limit so that we will know the strength of our character and the depth of our faith.

How deeply has your faith changed you? It's often only under extreme conditions that we find the answer to that question. To allow God to search you and know you is an intense exercise and not for the faint at heart. It can be dangerous to be known so intimately, and I am not so sure I want to see what needs to be dealt with in those deeper areas of who I am.

But notice what King David says in the closing verses of Psalm 139:24: "lead me along the path of everlasting life." You can be sure that enduring the dyno room of God's extreme testing will push you toward the limits of what life should really mean for you. The experiences of our earthly lives amount to more than a mere temporary existence; they prepare us for everlasting life. What a different outlook we would have if we would see our lives from God's eternal perspective.

Have you lost your way in the race of life? If a mechanic connected your "engine" to a dyno, you would discover a lot about your condition—specifically about the condition of your character, about some matters of routine maintenance, and about the areas of your life that need minor adjustments and the areas that need a complete overhaul. When you stop for a moment and connect with your Creator, read some Scripture and reflect, it is like you are connecting to a spiritual dyno. You may be frightened by the analysis, but remember that some of Jesus' favorite words while he walked on earth were "Fear not!" By his grace he is able to help you get your life back on track so that you find meaning and rest in him today.

## PIT NOTE

When you find the pain of living this life way out of proportion with the joy of it, look to God to help you through the trials. Cling to the biblical promise that God's purpose is to work things out for good—and to give you a hope-filled future (see Romans 8:28; Jeremiah 29:11). Learn to trust God through suffering, believing that the Spirit can use every experience to make you more like Jesus.

# 5

## PIT PRACTICE

> Under [Christ's] direction, the whole body is fitted together perfectly. As each part does its own special work, it helps the other parts grow, so that the whole body is healthy and growing and full of love.
>
> Ephesians 4:16

> Since we were restored to friendship with God by the death of his Son while we were still his enemies, we will certainly be delivered from eternal punishment by his life. So now we can rejoice in our wonderful new relationship with God—all because of what our Lord Jesus Christ has done for us in making us friends of God.
>
> Romans 5:10-11

The first stock car race my wife attended was with me at the Atlanta Motor Speedway. A die-hard Penn State football fan, she cared little for anything to do with racing. "Trust me!" I told her. "You come to this one event and you'll be hooked for life!" Well, she trusted me alright—and sat through what was one of the coldest finales in NASCAR history.

"I was impressed with one thing," she remarked later. "I couldn't believe how fast they serviced the car. The pit stops were really fun to watch—when I could see them through the frost on my eyelashes."

"For crying out loud!" I protested. "You've sat through college football games in Pennsylvania, just twenty miles below the Arctic Circle, and you're complaining about Atlanta in November."

She was undaunted. "That's different—football games are supposed to be cold—watching cars go around in circles should be done only in the summer. The pit stops were the only thing that kept my adrenaline going."

As I did my tour of duty in the sport, I was amazed to find many fans of the sport held similar sentiments. There is even a competition held during the NASCAR Sprint All-Star Challenge that pits crew against crew to crown the fastest service stops in the Cup series. Weekly practice sessions and workout regimens keep these teams in tip-top athletic and mental shape.

Matt Clark is the pit crew coach for the Hendrick Motorsports #48 team. This team not only won the NASCAR Sprint Cup Championship in 2006, but the pit crew honors as well. "Each week you will find us taking an afternoon outside the shop, practicing our stops," Matt says. "You want to average about thirteen seconds for a complete stop. So we have a practice car and run our strategies." I have witnessed these practices, and the crew members are very fluid in their motions and are diligent to observe details. Nothing is wasted.

Many teams record pit stops for later review, much like NFL coaches review game videos. They count the number of steps each pit crew member takes. Others actually graph the performance of each person on every pit stop.

NASCAR allows seven crew members "over the wall," but they perform their tasks as an extension of one another —as one. As the body of Christ at work in the world, we must treat our work with an equal amount of diligence and understanding that we are one in him. The apostle Paul goes to great lengths in his letter to the church at Ephesus to show believers that God is all about unity. It may be hard for you to think of yourself as an enemy of God (Romans 5:10-11), but that is what we all are apart from Jesus. When we look at the cross, we see more than just an act of divine love; we also see an act of divine wrath. God poured out judgment on his only Son for one reason: to reunite us with himself.

Because God has taken responsibility for this reconciliation and made us one with himself, we now have the ability to be as one with one another. It's the way we were meant to function. We are better together, and our differences complement one another and make us stronger. Similar to a NASCAR pit crew, believers are designed to function fluidly in union with Christ by our common faith and differing gifts. And just as the jack man needs the tire changers to finish the job, so is each role important as we serve and grow together as believers.

The walls we have to cross are at times much higher than those on pit road, and the stakes, of course, are much higher. God has given us a foundation from which we can operate in life as we were originally designed to do. One person cannot pit a race car. That's obvious! It should be equally obvious that a life lived by faith is done so alongside others. As believers around the world come together in places of worship on a regular basis, we participate together in the now and not yet. In one sense, our praise and worship are real time and important to our lives here, and in another sense, we are preparing for eternity, the place where we will live in a perpetual state of unhindered adoration of the God who brought us together through Jesus. If that is your desire, I am ready to go over the wall with you any day.

## PIT NOTE

How does the remark at the end of Romans 5:11 strike you? You can be a friend of God. Take a moment and look back over Romans 5:10-11. Thank the Lord for making this relationship with him possible. How should your friendship with God affect how you work with others?

# part 2

## OFF THE TRUCK

Very few teams unload at the track ready to go. No matter how they have tested themselves and their equipment in the weeks before the race, some real finesse work has to take place before a car can race competitively. A huge logistical endeavor is needed to move the equipment from place to place, and a team of suspension and engine specialists is needed to prepare the car. A race team must have the right people and the right commitment to run at the front.

Christ has given us the tools to progress in our walk with him throughout life. He intends for us to use these tools to serve and encourage one another along the way (Matthew 22:37-40). In doing so, we will come alongside one another and grow in our faith, maturing spiritually. The apostle Paul, writer of much of the New Testament, emphasizes throughout his letters the unity we have with God through faith in his only Son, Jesus. As a result of that unity, we have the stablest and most common ground for connection with one another (Ephesians 4:1-4; Philippians 2:1-4). Whether to accomplish the mission of winning races or of changing a community, a similar strategy must be employed. We bring a committed and unified team to any effort.

# 6

## UNSUNG HEROES

Jesus knew that the Father had given him authority over everything and that he had come from God and would return to God. So he got up from the table, took off his robe, wrapped a towel around his waist, and poured water into a basin. Then he began to wash the disciples' feet and to wipe them with the towel he had around him.

John 13:3-5

He sat down and called the twelve disciples over to him. Then he said, "Anyone who wants to be the first must take last place and be the servant of everyone else."

Mark 9:35

My friends Rodney and Kay Pickler retired after 2005. I am not sure they will ever know how much they meant to those of us who traveled the NASCAR Sprint Cup Series circuit. Rodney and Kay were drivers of another sort— a husband and wife team behind the wheel. In the work-a-day world of business, we would refer to them as "truckers." Year after year this couple crisscrossed the country, hauling the precious cargo of race cars, parts, electronics, and food. My first knowledge of Rodney came in 1992 when he was driving for the Joe Gibbs racing team, the number 18 hauler.

Remember that freezing cold race in Atlanta—the one I took my wife to and told you about in chapter 5? It was there that I saw Rodney Pickler clinch the Truck Driver Challenge award by putting an eighteen-wheeler through an obstacle course quickly and without mishap. This feat caused me to admire Rodney long before I met him. At that point, I had no idea that his wife often drove with him, and I wondered later, most amused, how she would have done in that competition. Kay is an excellent driver herself but prefers to be known for her hospitality more than for her prowess behind the wheel. "Ma Kay" makes the best Southern sweet tea ever, and I could always count on her for a glass of that liquid gold and a warm smile when I saw her. Often separated by hundreds of miles from my own mom, I was mothered by Kay more than I ministered to her. In the back of that transporter, she would give us a place to catch our breath, encourage us, and then send us back into the fray.

On the glamorous side of things, the men and women who drive the team transporters are often overlooked. This doesn't negate their service, however. They work in support of the crews and wear a variety of hats in serving them. If you find yourself equipped with a garage pass, you will notice the sights and smells behind each transporter. The various truck drivers who cook and clean for each team control that environment. Not only do they drive many hours and log several thousand miles each year, but they also keep the equipment clean and ready for visiting corporate sponsors and team owners. They keep the crews well fed as well.

Folks like Rodney and Kay are in racing for a reason they may not even be aware of. You see, most of these hardworking individuals are there because they love racing, want to make a living, and feel privileged to do so as a part of the NASCAR family. As a chaplain, however, I am glad they are there because of the example they set for all who would follow Jesus. The Rodneys and Kays of our sport lead others by being servants—just as Jesus did.

It is easy in the superstar-driven world of the Cup Series to feel a sense of entitlement. Everybody wants free stuff—free sunglasses, hats, food, beverages, apparel—the list goes on and on. In a world where everyone wants to be served, someone has to step up to the mic and declare, "That's not how you were designed to live!" On the night Jesus was betrayed, he took a basin of water and a towel, and like so many times before, showed his followers the power of paradox. He, the Lord of all creation, would kneel and perform the most menial and humbling task of washing the disciples' feet.

Does that image grip you? Can you hear the water splash and drip in the bowl as the one who made you prepares to wash you? I am overcome with emotion every time I mediate on this passage, and if I am not careful, I miss the importance of the lesson. If you and I internalize this too much, we absorb only the sense of awe at how Jesus served us. Like Peter, we must allow this even though it feels strange (John 13:6, 8). We would desire to wash the feet of Christ—that would seem more natural. If we close the lesson here, however, we lose the power of what Christ is teaching us. It is not merely about being clean (John 13:8). You and I, like Peter and the guys, must move toward serving one another as eagerly as we would wish to serve the Lord. In the view of Jesus, the servants are the greatest (Mark 9:35).

So as Rodney schlepped parts from transporter to garage and Ma Kay swept the entry and made tea, I was reminded each week that greatness comes from what many would say is the bottom up. As I reflect over my years of walking among this community, I find that I was most impacted for life by these drivers of another sort, for they were textbook examples of servanthood. They are the unsung heroes of racing, even as we are called to be the unsung heroes of God's kingdom.

Oh, by the way, may I pour you a glass of tea?

## PIT NOTE

When you are longing for your own creature comforts, ask Jesus to give you opportunities today to serve others the way he did. To be a hero in God's kingdom, we must stoop to become a servant-leader like Jesus.

# 7

## A VIEW FROM THE SPOTTER'S STAND

Remember your leaders who first taught you the word of God. Think of all the good that has come from their lives, and trust the Lord as they do.

Hebrews 13:7

"Son of man, I have appointed you as a watchman for Israel. Whenever you receive a message from me, pass it on to the people immediately."

Ezekiel 3:17

As I speak to various groups across this country, I'm surprised by how many people are NASCAR fans because they feel a personal connection with the sport. I have sat next to many an eager race fan who fully believed himself (and not infrequently, herself) capable of driving with the "big boys" around Daytona. Maybe it's because we dive into our cars each day for a morning commute to work—what's the big deal, right? After all, they're just driving faster, and the congestion is no worse than what we face on the freeway.

I hate to burst your bubble, but the aforementioned illusion is just that—the underestimation of a nation of shade-tree mechanics and Jiffy-Lubers. The speeds are so much faster than what one would expect, and the protective gear is in some ways very limiting. The drivers need an extra set of eyes. That is where the "spotters" come in.

You don't hear their names very often. Only those of us inside the garage on a weekly basis could identify them. Most spotters perform other tasks during the preparation stages of racing. Some are in the public relations field, others drive the family motor homes, some are the relatives of the asphalt pilots, and others are the owners of the teams. No matter what other roles they play or identities they possess, one thing remains common to them all: as spotters, they share the tremendous focus to keep a driver out of trouble. Over a specific radio frequency, the spotter is there to communicate things that the driver cannot see—whether behind, beside, or in front of him or her. The spotters do not speak until needed, but when they do speak, their words are not suggestions.

During practice sessions, the communication between the spotter and the driver is somewhat different than in a race. Teams usually get one-hour shots at perfecting their cars. There is therefore a tremendous amount of mad dashing to get on and off the track for adjustments. The spotter's trained eye carefully watches over the driver's entries and exits to make sure the passage is safe—and that the fine adjustments to the car are not hindered by an untimely crash with another eager competitor. To wreck a car in practice makes a team's weekend very long indeed and exacerbates a mental state that is already under stress.

In the spring of 2004, I took my first trip to the spotter's stand with a dear friend of mine. We were in Martinsville, and he wanted me to get a fresh perspective, quite literally a bird's-eye view, of what a practice session looked like from above. I was struck by the acceleration and braking that short track demanded of the drivers. It looked as if the drivers were pinned to the seat one second, then heading through the windshield the next—on the gas, on the brake, in constant rhythm from front stretch to back. The work looked exhausting—even for the spotter. As cars left the garage to enter the track, a major jam was caused by drivers waiting for the exact second to enter the herd of horsepower making laps. Spotters make the call to merge or not to merge. To tell you the truth, I wouldn't want the responsibility, but these guys understand their role and no one has to tell them how important they are.

After that Martinsville practice, my friend walked me back to the garage. He turned and said something I'll never forget. "You're kind of like a spotter. Know what I mean? You watch out for us, tell us the truth, and keep us out of trouble." I hadn't thought of that. He went on, "You know that job situation I was dealing with? You helped me see the wise thing to do, which wasn't exactly what I wanted to do. When the crash happened at work afterward, what you said helped me avoid getting caught up in the carnage."

"Man!" I told him. "That'll preach!"

Who is spotting for you in life? A wise driver will not go out on the track without someone watching out for him or her. Who is speaking into your life with words that are rooted in a love for you and a desire to see you reach your purpose and potential? Remember to thank those people, and keep them close.

And while we're on the subject, who are *you* spotting for? We all have a driver out there in life, perhaps a rookie of some sort, counting on us to lead them through blind spots. Keep your eyes open, stay focused, and speak timely words of caution, encouragement, and guidance in the race they are running.

## PIT NOTE

I heard pastor and author John Ortberg say that the higher you go in people's eyes, the less you'll hear the truth about yourself. Who in your life will always let you know when you're in danger, when you've run off track, or when you really need to make that pit stop? That person's honesty may be your greatest asset among friends.

# 8

## TRACK CONDITIONS

> "I have told you all this so that you may have peace in me. Here on earth you will have many trials and sorrows. But take heart, because I have overcome the world."
>
> John 16:33

My guess is that you did not check the surface temperature of the route you took to work today. You didn't consider whether a sudden cloud would block the sun before you made that turn to drop your child off at school this morning. The particular compound of the pavement didn't adversely affect the condition of the tires on your minivan. Such particulars seem ridiculous for us to consider in our everyday driving endeavors. But such conditions require tedious study for a race team.

Consider the historic speedway in Darlington, South Carolina. They don't call it "The Lady in Black" or "The Track Too Tough to Tame" just as a marketing strategy. Legendary crew chief Robbie Loomis told me early on that "you have to finish well at Darlington just to pay your tire bill." Its unique surface holds the environment of that coastal area—sand and sea shells. As Goodyear rubber rolls over this track at high speeds, those grinding indigenous properties slice through tires like a razor. The result is more pit stops and more adjustments. Even at short tracks like Loudon, teams could possibly get more than one hundred laps per set of tires, but at Darlington the pavement will chew up a set every forty laps. So teams not only compete against the horsepower and aero- dynamics of other teams, they also compete against the track environment.

Not only are there elements within the racing surface that affect these teams; there are also issues of temperature. On the superspeedways, track temperature can greatly affect the way a chassis is tweaked during practice. Since qualifying can take a lot of time at these tracks, adjust- ments are made in proportion to the time of day the cars will qualify. Just the slightest temperature variant can determine whether a car is loose or tight. I have stood beside my friend Ryan Newman, one of the best qualifiers in the sport, and heard him say, "Man, it's going to be hot when I have to make my run. It would be nice to have a cloud. Hear that, Dale? Ask God to give me a cloud."

A cloud over a hot track, especially over the turns at Daytona, Talladega, and Pocono, can cut a lap time by one or two tenths of a second. These critical shavings of time can put a car on the pole or out of the top ten starters. Worse, it could mean the difference between racing on Sunday and not "making the show." When the announcer says, "Drivers, start your engines," yours may be the big diesel of the team hauler before the long trip back home.

I don't have to convince you that the road we journey on through life is not a consistent and predictable path. Life is full of surprising potholes and various challenges that leave us feeling like we are losing control. Preachers call this the result of living in a fallen world, and these challenges leave us wondering if we have what it takes to make it.

Courage is based on trust. Race car drivers trust their crews to set up their cars to adjust properly to a particular track's idiosyncrasies. But there are times when drivers have to trust their own ability to do what they have trained for years to do—that is, they have to trust in the experience gathered during countless hours in the seat. Many times drivers have to "get up on the wheel" and drive with an extra measure of courage and conviction to win a race. Life gets that way sometimes as well.

For Christ to let us know that he has overcome the world provides us with a great source of strength. To think that he has kicked the locked door of death and the grave off its hinges to allow us access to eternal life demands our awe. You can thrive in the knowledge that you have been given the gift of a victorious position. You have what it takes, because Christ gave it to you. Using his adjustments, "get up on the wheel and drive."

## PIT NOTE

Do you lack confidence today? Take courage! You can face your circumstances because of Christ's victory. Ask the Holy Spirit to lead you into an empowered understanding of what you have been given through faith in the Lord Jesus.

# 9

## SANCTUARY PROVIDED BY GOODYEAR

Give a shepherd's care to God's flock among you, exercising oversight not merely as a duty but willingly under God's direction, not for shameful profit but eagerly. And do not lord it over those entrusted to you, but be examples to the flock.

1 Peter 5:2-3

[Christ] is the one who gave these gifts to the church: the apostles, the prophets, the evangelists, and the pastors and teachers. Their responsibility is to equip God's people to do his work and build up the church, the body of Christ.

Ephesians 4:11-12

The Goodyear Tire and Rubber Company holds the contract to supply racing teams with on-site service at each NASCAR racing venue. Every week Goodyear rigs roll in loaded with tires and equipment for a fresh start—and the blimp shows up every once in a while too. Tires and wheels are brought together, balanced, and stored at various locations around the track.

At this point, the "tire guys" for each team have the very important job of making sure that each tire is inflated to the correct pressure. (Interestingly, they use nitrogen instead of compressed air. This substitution keeps moisture out of the tire, which adds to the stability of air pressure within the tire.)

One of my mentors in track ministry challenged me to try his method of making personal contacts by using those towers of freshly prepared rubber. "Dale, if you will park yourself beside a stack of tires for one hour, you will be amazed by what happens. God will bring all sorts of crew members to you." You know what? He was exactly right. Why? Well, for the most part, everyone in the garage is busy, and it is tempting for a chaplain to get caught up in the activity. But if I looked as busy as those who worked in that environment, I would hear things like, "I saw you yesterday and wanted to talk but didn't want to bother you then," or "You look in a hurry today. Can I get with you later?" However, when I stood still in the shadow of those tires, watchful like a shepherd overseeing his flock, I became approachable. Like a water cooler in the office, five or six racing tires stacked on one another became a makeshift sanctuary for deeper conversation.

How does your walk with Christ contribute to a coworker's or friend's search for God? What value does a personal relationship with God serve in this life if we don't pass along what he teaches to those who have lost their way? Beside those rubber towers, sometimes surrounded by them, I have talked with men and women about all sorts of hurts and hang-ups. Even those who previously treated me with contempt have later huddled with me in prayer inside the safety of that canopy, looking for God in a place where most are looking for a show.

In his sermon "Message in the Stars," Frederick Buechner speaks to our need to transcend the daily grind and meet God in our work-a-day slices of life:

> For what we need to know, of course, is not just that God exists, not just that beyond the steely brightness of the stars there is a cosmic intelligence of some kind that keeps the whole show going, but that there is a God right here in the thick of our day by day lives who may not be writing messages about himself in the stars but in one way or another is trying to get messages through our blindness as we move around down here knee-deep in the fragrant muck and misery and marvel of the world. *It is not objective proof of God's existence that we want but the experience of God's presence. That is the miracle we are really after, and that is also, I think, the miracle that we really get.**

I emphasized the last part of Buechner's quote because I truly believe connection with God is a major common thread throughout humanity, crossing race and gender and class and culture. Deep down we truly believe that God is worthy of our purest loyalty, but where is he? We hunger for a divine audience and thirst for the pure nitrogen of the Holy Spirit to replace the dead air in our own lives. Where can we go to receive the Lord's resources? Those settings can come in a variety of places and fashions, maybe beside a stack of tires. So the next time you are watching forty-three race cars take the green flag, remind yourself that the rubber meeting the road may also have served somebody in gaining a grip on life.

**PIT NOTE**

Is there any part of your day when you *don't* look busy? How "approachable" are you—to your family, friends, coworkers, even strangers? What is your view of God— busy or at rest? Meditate for a few moments on Hebrews 4:9-11. What did you learn about God? What did you learn about yourself?

---

* Frederick Buechner, *The Magnificent Defeat* (New York: Seabury Press, 1975); italics mine.

# 10

## PLUG CHECK

> "Keep on asking, and you will be given what you ask for. Keep on looking, and you will find. Keep on knocking, and the door will be opened."
>
> Matthew 7:7

> The brothers sent Paul and Silas off to Berea ....[The Bereans] were more open-minded...for they eagerly received the message, examining the scriptures carefully every day to see if these things were so....Many of them believed.
>
> Acts 17:10-12, NET

Unlike the typical automobile of today, NASCAR race cars are not electronic fuel-injected vehicles. Their engines use an intake manifold to channel fuel and air from a carburetor to the cylinders below. The ignition used to explode the fuel in each cylinder is provided by a spark plug. This process of controlled detonation has always intrigued me. Within this "simple process" (the drivers' words, not mine!) lies the tremendous force called "horsepower."

Everyone I know loves that word. *Horsepower* has its roots in preindustrial days when workhorses were the most powerful source of movement available. The term came into use early on with mechanized prime movers to describe how much force was being exerted. Somewhere in history someone defined what it would look like to harness the power of workhorses. Engines were said to duplicate the power of a certain number of those horses to the wheels of a particular vehicle. All things being equal, in NASCAR that translates into about eight hundred equine energizers per vehicle.

If you have ever watched a car take its final lap during a practice session, you heard it scream down the backstretch under high rpm and shut off immediately. The driver had flipped the ignition switch to the "off" position and coasted for the rest of the return trip to the garage. This lap is called "the plug check."

It is not uncommon to see Jack Roush, founder, CEO, and co-owner of Roush Fenway Racing, personally inspecting a block of plugs after practice. I asked my friend Doug Yates, son of Robert and no novice engine man himself, to explain this process to me.

"Well, it's like this," he said. "You take this magnifying glass"—which looks like something the doctor would check your ears with—"and you carefully examine the textures and colors of the plugs. That evidence tells us if we need to adjust the carburetion for better results. Here, take a look."

I felt so important. But when I looked through the device, all I saw were slightly used plugs.

"What's *your* diagnosis?" Doug asked.

"They've been used," was all I could say, which was

exactly the answer he was expecting from me.

What Doug said next moved me deeply: "Now you know why we need your help to understand the Bible. Sometimes we don't see what you can clearly see."

The Word of God really is a treasure chest full of the revealed character of our Creator. My favorite seminary professor, John Hannah, reminded us often, "Men and women, press on to know the Lord! For you can know him truly. Not completely, mind you, but truly." Maybe you are just starting out on this journey and your Bible looks like that block of used spark plugs did to me. Keep looking! Keep asking! Keep searching!

In Matthew 7, Jesus is clear that those who search for truth will find it. For thirty years I have studied the Bible at various levels of maturity and understanding. This I can assure you: I have yet to close the book and say, "Okay, I have it all!" The older I get, the more I see as I read and receive the Bible's instruction. On this side of eternity, I gain from Scripture a greater reality than what I merely feel in this world. You too can search God's Word and start to believe that there really is more than the worst and best of this life. Look there again and again. Something fresh and insightful waits for your discovery every time you search.

## PIT NOTE

Laziness isn't only a physical thing. How often do you let others do your thinking for you? Even as you read this book, ask God to create in you a thirst to search the Scriptures for yourself. Expect God to reveal himself to you afresh.

# part 3

## HOW DID WE QUALIFY?

How you start isn't always indicative of how you will finish, but in racing, a team's qualifying position can often determine competitive ability. In racing you earn that track position by being the fastest car out there on your own. Drivers and teams will push the limits in every way possible to lay down the quickest lap around a particular track. Since every environment is different, adjustments must be made not just for track conditions, but also weather. Many factors go into one making the show on Sunday.

One of many paradoxes in the Christian life is that Jesus alone qualified us for this heavenbound race. He established our right standing with God by satisfying God's judgment with his death on the cross (Romans 5:6-11). We are called to "walk in a manner worthy" of that costly position Christ has secured for us (Ephesians 4:1, ESV).

# 11

## SMASHING ATOMS, SPLITTING SECONDS

Let us throw off everything that hinders and the sin that so easily entangles, and let us run with perseverance the race marked out for us.

Hebrews 12:1, NIV

We are citizens of heaven, where the Lord Jesus Christ lives. And we are eagerly waiting for him to return as our Savior.

Philippians 3:20

Assumptions, perceptions, and stereotypes—these three elements are dangerous to bring into your experience with any culture. Stock car racing is its own culture, filled with characters and heritage. By now you know I was no different from most casual observers of racing. We bring our own ideas about what goes on at the track and the people who work there. I projected my perception of everyone's background on them without intention. I assumed that these were Southern folk, superstitious but religious, simple but capable—and very polite! Imagine how convicted I felt when I met team members from all over this country with various ideologies and worldviews. Nothing shocked me more than meeting some brilliant PhDs in engineering.

Racing can be viewed from three perspectives, each connected to the others like the points on a triangle—horsepower, aerodynamics, and driver talent. Once a car goes out to qualify, these three things rise to the surface. And in recent years, full-blown technological masterminds have shown up on race teams to assist with the aerodynamic component. Unlike other racing vehicles, stock cars have the element of looking sort of like an everyday vehicle—and weighing like one too! These recognizable features are part of marketing the sport, but they also deliver a challenge to those who want to make them go fast. The engineers, or "atom smashers," as some crew members call them, classify this problem as "drag."

Drag occurs when the force of air meets restriction on the race car and slows it down. At the speeds we travel in our everyday lives, drag is not an issue for the morning commute—unless you are pushing a barn door down the highway! At racetrack speeds, and with the competition so tight, aerodynamics engineers earn their pay by finding the edge between enough down-force to hold a car on the track but not so much that it decreases the qualifying lap time. If you doubt that aerodynamic finesse matters, don't take my word for it. In 2000 I heard veteran driver (and amateur comedian) Jeff Burton blame a bug on his windshield for keeping him from winning the pole position! This thing called drag can keep you from reaching your potential.

Drag in your spiritual life can bring a ton of frustration. When you first start out following Christ, you may feel superhuman, able to defeat any and all temptations. It doesn't take long, however, until you realize you're not bulletproof. As we walk with the Lord on this side of heaven, we make our way through a life where we will never completely feel at home. The apostle Paul reminds us that our citizenship is in heaven (Philippians 3:20). With that being the case, we need to wake up to the reality that we are in this world but no longer bound to it.

Press on through those defeats that you feel disqualify you from the love of God. You were qualified, restored to the relationship you were intended to have with him, by the death and resurrection of the Lord Jesus. Have you reached a place where you can believe this? If so, press on through the stuff that drags you down. The secrets you keep will have control over you as long as you keep them secret. Invite others you trust to form a safe place to disclose the drag in your life.

As you continue to follow Jesus, and with the help of your traveling companions, you will start to break free from the sin that keeps you defeated. As long as we are this far from home, our common enemy, the devil, will continually remind us of just how far we have to go. He will tell you that you don't have what it takes to make it. On this journey we look through a windshield plastered and scarred with signs of failure, injustice, and sins too many to number. Christ is here to clear the view so that we can see him in our daily lives. As long as you stay behind the Leader, the bugs on your windshield do not have to slow you down.

## PIT NOTE

What secret sin do you work to keep hidden? The power of that secret doesn't have to control your life. Ask the Lord now to show you someone to help you carry the shame or guilt of it. Doing so will break the controlling power of the secret.

# 12

## QUIET CONFIDENCE

Blessed is the God and Father of our Lord Jesus Christ, who has blessed us with every spiritual blessing in the heavenly realms in Christ. For he chose us in Christ before the foundation of the world that we may be holy and unblemished in his sight in love.

Ephesians 1:3, NET

Therefore since we have a great high priest who has passed through the heavens, Jesus the Son of God, let us hold fast to our confession. For we do not have a high priest incapable of sympathizing with our weaknesses, but one who has been tempted in every way just as we are, yet without sin. Therefore let us confidently approach the throne of grace to receive mercy and find grace whenever we need help.

Hebrews 4:14-16, NET

When you think of drivers like Michael Waltrip, Jeff Gordon, and Jimmie Johnson, you can't help thinking about the warmth of their personalities. They enjoy talking about all sorts of life issues, and they will surprise you with their scope of knowledge beyond racing. Put any of these guys in front of a camera or an audience, and they can be conversational and engaging. In the moments before qualifying, however, they put on their "game faces." Focused and intense, they have no time for chitchat—these men are on a mission to lay down the fastest lap in the field. Their warm and fuzzy countenances disappear.

Don't mistake the intensity you see on a driver's face before qualifying as fear; rather, it is a look of confidence to do the task at hand. Tony Stewart once told me to come visit him "in my office"—which meant for me to come by and see him after he buckled in for his run. As you would not approach your boss's office without invitation for fear of disturbing his or her personal work, no one approaches the seat of a race car without a certain respect for what is going on. The more confidence drivers have in their teams and vehicles, the more at rest they are in their own abilities to put the car on the edge of its fullest potential.

Garage legend has it that the great Dale Earnhardt was calmest when he was buckled into his Goodwrench machine. Doctors monitoring his heart rate reported that Earnhardt's pulse *slowed down* just before he climbed into a car. Should we interpret this as carelessness? Never. Not complacency, but confidence, made Dale one of the greatest race car drivers ever. He had a confidence that didn't boast—he didn't have to speak what was already shown during the race.

One day I stood next to Dale at the end of the front stretch, just the two of us, as his son took his first qualifying lap around the challenging Pocono raceway. As Dale Jr came by us at top speed, he charged down the front stretch through turns one and two on his way to the backstretch. Big E turned to me and asked, "What'cha think, Dale? Did he let off?" Without hesitation I replied, "I certainly would have!" It was the first time I made him laugh—even though I was serious! Naturally, he wouldn't have let off, and he didn't think that Dale Jr should either. By the look of pride on his face, I don't think he believed Dale Jr slowed at all. Why would he? Going flat out is what race car drivers do.

Every top driver who has climbed behind a wheel has a sense of being out of place when not behind the wheel. That environment of seat, roll-cage, and toggle switches feels like the spot created for them to hold. God has given us the same privilege of being before him—not in a come and go sense, but in a setting of permanence and rest. We enjoy this privilege not just after we die, but now by an intimate connection with him every moment of every day (Hebrews 4:16). You may trust God with all the historical stuff in the Bible, things that happened in the past, but how is your confidence in what he says about you right now? In what state of mind do you move through all the challenging circumstances that orbit around you? God is not just a God of the past; he is the God of eternity—his eternity—and you are invited to be with him every day. Live in that strength.

## PIT NOTE

Our connection with God is moment by moment, and as disciples of Jesus, we have the privilege of walking with him through out days. Have confidence as you bring your requests before the Lord. Don't be afraid! God invites us to come—and celebrates when we do.

# 13

## NO FEAR

> There is no fear in love, but perfect love drives out fear, because fear has to do with punishment. The one who fears punishment has not been perfected in love.
>
> 1 John 4:18, NET

> God did not give us a Spirit of fear but of power and love and self-control.
>
> 2 Timothy 1:7, NET

No matter the circumstances, Bill Elliott makes me smile. Even after a funeral service, I have stood next to Bill and listened to him tell stories about himself and the deceased. He exudes a healthy amount of gratitude and sense of humor when he tells a story. His command of imagery combined with his Georgia drawl and "aw shucks" nature compels those within earshot to listen. The comfort level one feels around him is disarming. No wonder the fullness of his character and talents sneak up on you. It may shock some people who see him only as a racer to learn that Bill is an accomplished pilot and snowboarder. He is like a real-life Andy Griffith, full of wit, wisdom, and life experience.

I remember the first time I met Bill, he was talking with some folks a couple of hours before qualifying. "Bill, what's it like to qualify one of these cars for a race?" I asked.

He smiled and asked me, "You ever driven on ice before?"

"Oh yes!" I answered.

"Well, imagine what that would feel like out there. You're trying to go as fast as you can without losing control of the car. It's a very fine line."

Even now when Bill and I are together at the track, he will walk up to me just before qualifying and elbow me in the arm: "Got your car ready for you." That is my invitation—tongue in cheek—to climb in for the lap of my life. Of course, even a dauntless competitor like Bill has a sober frame of mind for what he is about to do. Joking a little about it simply takes some of the edge off the anxiety.

I expect that most of us have a more-than-subtle respect for speed. Having traveled little in excess of the posted speed limits, the notion of touching 200 miles per hour is both alluring and terrifying—with terror holding the upper hand for most of us. The Greeks had a specific word they used for the way their "gut" ached in specific situations. We use a form of that expression when we say things like "He has guts to go over there" or "She made a gutsy move in that situation." We know what it is like to have our guts compel us to risk involvement in a frightening situation, usually out of compassion or empathy. Do we, however, have the guts to hurl ourselves around an oval at a high rate of speed for sheer drive to be first? I, for one, do not have that ability. Courage is, obviously, relative to the "guts" of one's own constitution.

Living in a world where the cliff of fear is a regular part of everyone's terrain, we should not be surprised that Jesus often told his followers, "Fear not." We meet people and situations head-on in a variety of intimidating circumstances. No wonder we creatively look for places to duck and hide. Fear is so common an emotion for us that we react to it subconsciously. How then can a relationship with God possibly dispel our fears?

In his first letter, the apostle John ties our fears to punishment or some negative action on the part of another toward us (1 John 4:18). We are forced to come to terms with the notion that if there truly is a divine being who created us, then we must be accountable to him—and wonder if we can trust him, just as Lucy questions Mr. Beaver in Narnia, "Is [Aslan] safe?" She wonders if this great king, who is portrayed in the story by a lion, is one she can trust. Mr. Beaver's response is quite insightful when comparing a meeting with Aslan to experiencing the vast majesty and power of God. Aslan is most certainly not safe—what lion would be?—but more important, he is good.

The Bible assures us that no matter what our circumstances, God is good. Like a banzai lap on the icy road of life, we don't often feel safe in this world. But we follow a God who calls us his children, and this should compel us to stay close to the Lord. No longer separated from God, we have no reason to fear, but rather to sense the power to say no to sin and yes to loving others (2 Timothy 1:7).

## PIT NOTE

What do you fear most in life? Failure? Rejection? Disclosure? The unknown? Take your Bible and read Mark 4:35-41. What was Jesus leading his followers to believe? In your specific situation or storm, where do you think he wants to lead you? If he doesn't calm your storm, he will calm you.

# 14

## HIT THE ENTRY POINT

Acknowledge that the LORD is God! He made us, and we are his. We are his people, the sheep of his pasture. Enter his gates with thanksgiving; go into his courts with praise. Give thanks to him and bless his name.

Psalm 100:3-4

Who may climb the mountain of the LORD? Who may stand in his holy place? Only those whose hands and hearts are pure.

Psalm 24:3-4

My friend Ryan Newman is a great qualifier. The "Rocket Man" is an almost perfect blend of guts and gray matter. With a BS in engineering from Purdue University, Ryan sets the example of what is most valued in today's drivers. He has the ability to analyze the experiential feel of driving and communicate that knowledge effectively with the guys who work on the hardware. Ryan was the first driver to educate me on the irreplaceable value of "hitting your entry points." One way to ensure a great qualifying run is to consider your approach into a turn on the racetrack. Seconds can be added or removed from a lap according to the way a driver manages the turns.

The challenge for every race team is to set up the car so that it can maneuver through the turns as quickly as possible. A "push" means that the car wants to go up the racetrack toward the wall. Very bad. To be "loose" means that the car wants to break free from the track at the back end, resulting in what we call a "spin out." Also very bad. Drivers must go into a turn at the optimum level of entry where they can carry and maintain the most speed without losing the car in a spin or plowing into the wall from the front. Drivers' talent can often be measured in how well they hit those marks. Ryan Newman does this well because he carefully considers his approach to those turns before he engages them.

Something that prevents us from a vibrant life with God is that we often do not know how to approach him. Do we fear God the way we do a dark alley or an IRS audit? Do we expect a relationship that is similar to a visit with our grandparents or a phone call to a friend? If the answer is "yes" to either of those questions, we should reconsider our entry point. I love how contemporary Christian singer Nichole Nordeman describes this tension in her song "Tremble." She wonders if she has entered God's presence too casually. She thinks maybe there's something she has neglected or overlooked. How do we approach God informally, familiarly, and yet preserve the holy quality we call "sacred"? As she describes the privilege of gaining of attention from the risen Lord, she considers her entry point with a reminder: "Let me not forget to tremble."*

I once asked Ryan to give a talk with me to a church group in the Charlotte area. He didn't describe his anxiety about this in terms of flat-out speed per se, but in terms of that speed under the shifting duress of a subtle on-track maneuver. "Beav', when you're ready to take a qualifying lap all the way through turn four at Michigan, I'll be ready to do a speech with you in a church setting." To me there was no comparison, but I guess we all have our comfort—and discomfort—levels. To him, the sacred essence of speaking about God and faith were more frightening than a turn at 200 miles per hour.

Maybe we need to evaluate the cavalier attitude we take at times in our thoughts of God. The Lord is not a vending machine with a variety of satisfaction available to us with the convenient push of a button. Even as God's children, we need to have a level of respect, reverence, and awe that divine character commands. We approach God confidently, to be sure, but also more reverently as we start to understand his greatness. Don't be surprised if you often feel strangely drawn to yet also repelled by the wooing presence of God in your life. To think that the one who spanned light years of universe with his hand (Isaiah 40:12) also knows the number of hairs on your head (Matthew 10:30; Luke 12:7) can be a little unsettling. It's healthy to consider the one who cannot be fully considered. May we approach the Lord with the level of respect he is due—with gratitude and hearts that are devoted to God's will.

## PIT NOTE

How do you enter God's presence? Do you possess the right balance of awe and ease? I encourage you to find and listen to the lyrics of Nichole Nordeman's song "Tremble." Take some time to think about the message.

*Nichole Nordeman, "Tremble," from the album *This Mystery* (Sparrow, 2003).

# 15

## DISQUALIFIED

Remember that in a race everyone runs, but only one person gets the prize. You also must run in such a way that you will win. All athletes practice strict self-control. They do it to win a prize that will fade away, but we do it for an eternal prize. So I run straight to the goal with purpose in every step. I am not like a boxer who misses his punches. I discipline my body like an athlete, training it to do what it should. Otherwise, I fear that after preaching to others I myself might be disqualified.

1 Corinthians 9:24-27

We are his workmanship, having been created in Christ Jesus for good works that God prepared beforehand so we may do them.

Ephesians 2:10

One of the most difficult things a race chaplain does on a consistent basis is visit with the teams who pack up and go home after the qualifying trials. For some reason, these teams miss the race, and that can be very disheartening after working a fourteen-hour day. Nobody wants to go home, but with only forty-three spots and sometimes fifty-plus cars…? You can do the math. After the qualifying trials, the chaplain can often be seen walking slowly through the crowd of homebound crews offering encouragement to those who want it. It is always a sad sight to see a loading ramp close on the back of a hauler before race day.

Perhaps most discouraging to me are the teams caught cheating to increase their qualifying speeds. I've never really understood how this can happen with inspectors hovering around the garage all the time. And although I have addressed the subject in our prerace chapel services, I have never been invited to discuss the subject with those of influence. Everything appears to be done above the line of misconduct, but when fines and suspensions are handed down, it becomes obvious that someone has been acting dishonestly. This type of thing makes the sport look like a sham, and parents trying to raise their kids with integrity will not follow a sport in which influences are not virtuous. Since many of the drivers have their families with them at the track, they too field questions from their children when such issues are raised in the sport.

In my job as a pastor, I am expected to be a man of authenticity and virtue. I am content with those expectations existing alongside my calling, and I appreciate the accountability. But shouldn't those standards be equally pressed upon us all, no matter what our profession in this world—mechanic, millwright, or medical professional? I think so. The great adventure in following Christ is that he calls us to live a higher, nobler life.

Doesn't that calling to live on a higher level, where success and riches are defined in terms of character and selflessness, captivate us all? Come on, I mean, really—who can watch some sort of devastation in the world, even in a place where you have never been, and not want to make a difference? I am completely convinced that those who rise up with a passion to impact those situations for good do so because of the image of God within them. It is also God's image in us that compels us to live ethically in our families and business communities. We have the imprint of our Creator on our souls, and that mark will always war with ideas that, while accepted by the masses, are not in God's holy character. This struggle is frustrating, and even when we choose to do right, the choice is usually unsatisfying in the near term. It is easier to go the way of the world, and if you are like me, sometimes you do. I have grieved many lost opportunities to do things God's way, and I wonder what I have missed because of my errors.

Thankfully, in the race of life we have been given the perfect qualifications of a right standing with God through Jesus Christ. His perfect substitution on our behalf brings us into a relationship with God we did not enjoy until we accepted his sacrifice for our sins. We cannot earn our way into God's favor, but since Christ has attained God's favor for us, we can choose each day to live our lives as an offering to him. In 1 Corinthians 9 we see that it is through self-control that we stay in the race. Our salvation has no benefit to others if they do not see a radical difference in our behavior. Christ-followers grow more and more like Christ, taking on his characters. It's his character that people see when we are at a normal flow of life—at work, school, home, and play.

The ability to exercise self-control over our selfish desires and ill temper will display a supernatural character to the world. Without it we demonstrate a life that is devoid of the kind of "workmanship" Christ is intent on completing in those who follow him (Ephesians 2:10, NIV). It is often the slightest cracks in our character that can lead to catastrophic downfalls. We therefore line up with the competitors, if you will, but go home early. By faith, Christ has qualified you to run, so don't take yourself out of the race. Instead, set the pace so that others may follow.

## PIT NOTE

How often do you react in ways that speak a faithless life, a rebellious life, to those who watch you? Each one of us must submit our lives to God's authority if we hope to produce a life that is consistent with Christ's character.

# part 4

## FINAL INSPECTION

Every race car goes through one final inspection before the green flag flies and the thunder rolls. During this inspection everything is rechecked to make sure that the essentials are maintained and working. Checklists are plastered to the car's body in different areas of responsibility. Crew members sign their names to these lists, indicating that they have tightened screws or cleaned parts. These procedures have as much to do with safety as with performance. To keep consistent with the rules of NASCAR, teams also push their vehicles through the official inspection bay one last time.

As followers of Christ, we too must exercise our lives with disciplines that keep us on the right track (1 Corinthians 9:27). Bible study, prayer, Scripture memorization, and corporate worship time will aid us in developing a consistent daily faithfulness to follow our Lord (Ezra 7:10). Whether we are new to the faith or have been believers for a while, we need to be sharpening our discipleship disciplines, for it is a lifelong process. If Christ has made us qualified to run, he is also at work within to keep us in the race (Philippians 1:6).

# 16

## CHILD'S PLAY

One day some parents brought their children to Jesus so he could touch them and bless them, but the disciples told them not to bother him. But when Jesus saw what was happening, he was very displeased with his disciples. He said to them, "Let the children come to me. Don't stop them! For the Kingdom of God belongs to such as these. I assure you, anyone who doesn't have their kind of faith will never get into the Kingdom of God." Then he took the children into his arms and placed his hands on their heads and blessed them.

Mark 10:13-16

It is impossible to please God without faith. Anyone who wants to come to him must believe that there is a God and that he rewards those who sincerely seek him.

Hebrews 11:6

Jeff Gordon has already attained the marks of an extraordinary career. He has won the most coveted events in NASCAR and enjoys multiple championship rings in his jewelry box. He recently tied and then surpassed the late Dale Earnhardt in number of races won—a feat very unpopular with Junior fans by the way! Jeff was five years old when he started with a passion for the sport, and he has not slowed down. He has been so focused and dedicated to the sport of auto racing that one might imagine he could do little else. At least, that is what I used to think!

For the teams that qualify (and Jeff usually does!), there can be a tremendous time of relaxation after each qualifying round. Drivers can be found playing with their kids or walking their dogs in the evenings. Sometimes they have their own team over for a cookout. Matt Kenseth can grill some mean Wisconsin Brats. Ryan Newman might fry some fish he caught the weekend before. In New Hampshire we can always count on the rich smell of boiled lobsters coming from somebody's motor coach spot. And sometimes a driver will meet with the chaplain for conversation that goes beyond spring rates and corner weights.

At the Southern 500 in Darlington a few years ago, I grilled a couple of steaks and had Jeff over to my motor home for supper and a game of chess. I had heard that he was "good at chess" but thought he would not be much of a challenge. After all, he was just a race car driver. I was wrong. He schooled me like a master and was humble about it. I was stunned—not that he was humble, but that he was so good at chess. Chess for crying out loud!

After the meal we talked about some deeper issues of life and were about to wind up our time together when my young son burst into the room. Here was my six-year-old son standing next to a famous race car driver. Most kids his age would have mumbled and fumbled, produced something for Jeff to autograph, and hung around until making an uncomfortable exit. But in this moment, Jeff was just someone who stood in the way of my son's mission. A boy needed his father. He never took his eyes off me, acknowledged Jeff with only a "Hey," and immediately raised a damaged plastic action figure to my attention. "Dad, I really need you to fix this…if you would…please?"

Jeff and I have never revisited that event, but I think he was amazed. Not only was this kid interrupting an interaction between a celebrity driver and another adult, but the boy was more interested in the average adult than the celebrity! The encounter amused me, but it also made me think about a Gospel story about a childish interruption of adult business.

When the little children of Jesus' day wanted an audience with him, the disciples responded as any grown-up would: "Don't bother the Master!" Jesus set the disciples straight and invited the children in for a chat. Jesus informs us that the kingdom of heaven is made up of people who approach God in the way of a child. Certainly there is an element of dependency on the part of a child that any loving parent would welcome, but I think that there is something else. I think Jesus is showing us that children have the audacity, the boldness, to approach him with confidence.

Children walk into a room as if they are expected! Oh that we grown-ups would be as sure of Christ's love and as bold to have an audience with him. Certainly my son will mature. His social graces will be sharpened. His sensitivity to important conversations will blunt his brashness.

But like our heavenly Father, earthly dads will always want their children to be certain of their love and acceptance.

## PIT NOTE

Think of the people you love the most. How much do you enjoy being with them? Do you think God enjoys you that much? He does!

# 17

## DISCIPLE-ADE

Jesus replied, "People soon become thirsty again after drinking this water. But the water I give them takes away thirst altogether. It becomes a perpetual spring within them, giving them eternal life."

John 4:13-14

How can one say that a person sitting behind a steering wheel is truly an athlete? Most will admit that the pit crews exert enough sprintlike energy to correlate what they do with track and field sports, but everything else looks pretty easy. I mean, really, how much energy does it take to shift gears every now and then?

I will admit that for a while I too scoffed to think of the guys who drive race cars as real athletes. I grew up playing baseball and football. No one ever questioned what qualified those sports as athletics. The people who played those sports were athletes, and they were treated and trained as such. Race car drivers seem different because they are not throwing or running or hitting each other—not outside the car anyway.

Veteran racer Jimmy Spencer, Mr. Excitement himself, told me that he could lose more than ten pounds during a race. I was stunned! After that particular conversation, every driver I asked admitted that he also lost a significant percentage of weight during a race. Several drivers are now trying to figure out ways to load up on fluids and maintain a more adequate level during the days before and after a race. Jimmie Johnson once told me that if he waits until the day before a race to hydrate—or even two days before—he pays for it dearly come Monday. Most guys I spoke with about this issue start to monitor their intake carefully four days before a race. Hydration is a critical component to life in general, but it is especially important to the life of an athlete—athletes such as race car drivers.

My friend Eric, an athletic trainer who has worked with race car drivers and athletes from various other sports, has told me that once an athlete loses more than 2 percent of body weight in water, reflexes and reaction capabilities begin to slow. That is a real problem for a race car driver, even more so than for most traditional stick and ball sport players. You see, the more water a race car driver loses, the more of a danger he becomes to those competing against him. Water is essential to keeping drivers safe on the race-track. This being so, come race morning, drivers had better have the necessary fluids already in them.

You might be surprised to know that your own body is comprised of two-thirds liquid. We all need $H_2O$ to live. Jesus captured this image in a spiritual way during a conversation with a woman in the land of Samaria. Journeying through that land, he stopped by a well during the heat of the day and met a woman coming to draw water. What made this particularly strange was that women didn't normally make their water runs at this time of the day. They came in groups to the well much earlier. We get the idea that she came at this time because she wanted to be alone.

Through divine insight, Jesus told this woman everything about herself. He revealed to her that she was looking for fulfillment in the wrong places. "Drink from me and you will never thirst again," he said. "Sir, give me this water," she implored (see John 4:14-15). She wanted living water so she wouldn't have to keep going to the well. What he offered was a life source of spiritual water that flowed freely from within. This water didn't have to be drawn or carried, simply possessed.

The writer tells us that the woman ran back into town and told everyone about the man she had met (John 4:29). Could she have been so full of this new life source that the townspeople would have wondered who she was? Maybe it was the first time she had felt the freedom to address her community. When a person is full of living water, he or she bubbles over—and why not? This woman was fully hydrated after a long draught.

I am awed by a small detail the apostle John gives us in the account. When the woman left the well to go back into town, she didn't take her water jar with her (John 4:28). I believe John notes this to reinforce another lesson. Yes, our bodies will needs lots of $H_2O$ in the days to come, but the wellspring of life has been tapped. The vessels we would use to catch significance are no longer necessary. The water that Christ provides cannot be contained in those devices. On the contrary, Jesus has filled our lives with meaning. Earthly apparatuses cannot contain such a resource.

If you are following Jesus, you have a daily supply of his water for your soul. Unlike the drivers who need a leverage sponsor to supply the team with intervals that peak on the hottest weekends, our Sponsor produces refreshment continually. In a world where holes are kicked in our hearts and we leak, Christ offers a flow of his grace and peace. The water of life, Jesus Christ, is there for us daily. Drink deeply.

## PIT NOTE

What have you identified that is most lacking in your life? Could you have made a misdiagnosis, when what you really need is the water of life? Reread John 4. What effects did the Lord's water have on this woman?

# 18

## OUT OF THE WRECKAGE

> Once you were dead, doomed forever because of your many sins. You used to live just like the rest of the world, full of sin, obeying Satan, the mighty prince of the power of the air....But God is so rich in mercy, and he loved us so very much, that even while we were dead because of our sins, he gave us life when he raised Christ from the dead....For he raised us from the dead along with Christ, and we are seated with him in the heavenly realms.
>
> Ephesians 2:1-7

I don't remember the date. In NASCAR dates are expressed in the season of the year and the geography of the show. It was the fall of 2002, and we were remembering the tragedy of 9/11. Frankly, the sport had had a lot to grieve about over the past few years. The terrorist attack on the World Trade Center just continued the thread in an overwhelming way. The whole world continued to blur through the fire and smoke. We were in Dover, Delaware—one year later.

I was walking as I always do through the garage where my congregation works incessantly to prepare cars for race day. In the bright noonday sun, hazed by the fumes of all the open exhausts, a young man walked up to me and introduced himself. He was Doug Macmillan, the best friend of Todd Beamer, the "Let's roll" guy of Flight 93.

"They tell me you're the pastor here and that you travel with these celebrities all year long" was his opening statement. "I hope that doesn't get me in any trouble" was my response. "How have these guys responded to you over the past year?" was his question. "They've been more attentive. Done more soul searching. Trashed a lot of stuff that doesn't mean much. I'm afraid that stuff will find its way back home after a while though, and they'll stop being so attentive to what God is saying to them."

"I want to show you something that might be of service to you in the future," Doug said. "Hold out your hand." With some reservation, I complied. Doug produced a small, purple velvet bag and emptied the contents into my open palm. At first I simply thought it was a small piece of scrap metal, heavy and ugly. But then I noticed it was a watch, or more accurately, what was left of one. I could make out part of an *R*, the bottom of an *E*, and most of an *X*. At that point I new it was a severely beaten corpse of a Rolex.

Doug saw me figure this out, and then he said, "You're holding all that's left of my best friend. It was found in the wreckage of Flight 93." He turned the piece over and showed me enough of the serial number that matched Todd's registration card after he bought it. "Todd bought this thing in celebration of what he'd accomplished in his career. It was his prized possession, and now it's nothing but scrap. You tell your guys, Dale—you tell them none of this stuff matters. It's all gonna end up in the wreckage."

I'd all but forgotten about this conversation. It was lost among all the memorable exchanges I had in those garages. But from time to time, like you I'm hurled into the memory of all that happened on 9/11. Recalling the heroism of Todd and those folks on that doomed plane, my aging memory coughed this up for review. It helps me keep things in perspective. Beyond the materialism of life, above it actually, are the things that matter most—trusting God's sovereignty, serving my family as a father and husband, sharing my heart with friends, and growing deep in Jesus. Those are the things that go beyond the wreckage for me. What about you?

Do you understand that humankind isn't treading water in a sea of sin? We are dead in it. Helpless (Ephesians 2:1). We were not designed to reduce life to a search for value among the best of the wreckage. Through faith in Christ, God pulls us from the wreckage and places us in a situation of life as it was truly intended to be experienced—in "the incredible wealth of his favor and kindness" (Ephesians 2:6-7). If that has been your experience, do not forget who you are and the valuable treasure you possess.

## PIT NOTE

What kind of stuff is important to you? How often have you been forced to acknowledge that such stuff isn't, in fact, important at all? Ask God to lead you into the truth that this world is not our home, that our stuff really belongs to God—just as we do. Try to remember that what matters most on earth is that you live so you may fully enjoy what matters most in heaven.

# 19

## GARAGE TALK

Don't you realize that all of you together are the temple of God and that the Spirit of God lives in you?

1 Corinthians 3:16

The electricity in the race day air is more than addictive—it is downright hypnotic! Typically I rise early on those mornings to gather a group of television production workers for a predawn devotion and prayer service. These hardworking people put on the show that race fans are accustomed to viewing from their living rooms. Robotic camera operators like Dan Belue, technicians and truck drivers with nicknames like Turtle, Kranky, T-Bone, and Uncle Fester gather with me in a graphics trailer driven from track to track by my buddy Ron. For a few moments we recognize God's presence with us, pray for each other, and read a portion of Holy Scripture.

As the morning moves along, I walk back into the garage and post chapel notices as a reminder to everyone who can take a few moments from final preparations that we will meet in our normal time and place. Two hours before every race, NASCAR requires every driver and crew chief to meet for a short meeting to go over the particular situations leading up to as well as getting through the actual racing event. This meeting (officiated by the race director, David Hoots) is usually held in either a media center or in an empty section of the garage. In Pocono, Pennsylvania, for instance, we meet in an area marking the entrance to the garage named in memory of Adam Petty. In Bristol, Tennessee, we have a special room behind the Goodyear tire shop. In Loudon, New Hampshire, we meet in the garage spaces left empty by the companion series that raced the day before. In Daytona, it is usually Garage C. Every track has a definitive place, but for many of us, it doesn't define where we hold the drivers' meeting—it is where we worship!

To conclude the meeting, David asks me to close in prayer. At this point, the community is allowed to attend a short worship service, sponsored by Motor Racing Outreach (MRO), the motorsports ministry that commissions chaplains and other ministry workers in the racing community. I look forward to that worship service all week. It feels like the only place where this community meets in unity and on common ground. From Ryan and Krissie Newman who sit on the front row and Jimmie and Chandra Johnson behind them—the Kenseths are always on the back row, a point I fuss to Matt about on occasion—to Fred and Brenda Lockman, a retired couple who travel the circuit and work with NASCAR, a variety of team members and officials gather to hear the Word of God preached and to pray. It is the time that God reminds us all collectively that we are under his authority, and as we respond to that authority obediently, we are therefore under God's blessing. I am passionate about the ministry of Motor Racing Outreach and their privileged facilitation of this gathering of worship each week—the same congregation in a different place for the same reason.

Hopefully your weekly corporate worship experience is

at least this engaging. You *are* meeting with others regularly, aren't you? Let's face it, getting together with a group of others and seeking the Lord to worship him can be challenging. But according to Scripture, it is essential to the health and growth of our spiritual lives. The Old Testament examples speak to the need for assembly in the temple, the place God had authorized for worship, complete with preachers and worship leaders—the priests and Levites. In the New Testament, the writer to the Hebrews admonishes us this way: "Let us take thought of how to spur one another on to love and good works, not abandoning our own meetings, as some are in the habit of doing, but encouraging each other, and even more so because you see the day drawing near" (Hebrews 10:24-25, NET).

I have learned that God can show up in some pretty strange places, and with our bodies being the very house of his Spirit, why shouldn't he show up in those places? Far too many part-time followers of Christ divorce him on Monday mornings—this is not living in a "manner worthy of the calling to which you have been called" (Ephesians 4:1, ESV). My desire for you is to live your life as an extended worship service. Be an extended day of worship throughout your week, sanctifying moments at work and in your home. Remember that Christ is with you wherever you go—even before you start the race day.

## PIT NOTE

Have you thought much about your life at work and home as an act of worship? It can be. When you live your life as a follower of Jesus, life becomes a moment offering to him. Where can you incorporate this in your family and work life?

# 20

## WAR WAGONS AND CRASH CARTS

The LORD is close to the brokenhearted; he rescues those who are crushed in spirit.

Psalm 34:18

The Spirit of the Sovereign LORD is upon me, because the LORD has appointed me to bring good news to the poor. He has sent me to comfort the brokenhearted and to announce that captives will be released and prisoners will be freed.

Isaiah 61:1

The final preparations before the thunder rolls consist of mobile communication centers (called "war wagons") and repair facilities being brought into a small area near pit road. Each team has a pit stall in which to service and maintain their race car throughout the race. Each pit stall becomes an emergency room for race cars.

Time after time I have seen crew members take a wrecked race car and do the miraculous. So before each race, the guys go over what they think would be needed in a crash situation and cart it out to pit road. Saws, hammers, rivets, and lots and lots of duct tape are only part of what goes into these automotive first-aid kits—otherwise known as crash carts. A can of ether is critical in case the engine stalls. You probably have many memories of your favorite team pushing their car down pit road with one guy simultaneously spraying shots of starter fluid in the gaps between windshield and hood.

In a race where points for making laps add up to dollars, everything within NASCAR law is done to maintain the minimum required speed. Did you know that? It's true. Kasey Kahne could qualify his car on the pole, but if he fails to maintain a predetermined speed throughout the race, even after an incident, the car has to be parked. Puttering along the apron of the racetrack is not an option. Hopefully those pit-stop paramedics Kasey calls his "guys" can restore the race car fast enough to be, well, fast enough.

To compete in and complete every race, a driver has to have faith in the abilities of the entire team. The symbiotic chemistry between the driver on the track and the crew in the pits often determines a championship season. I understand that for the race fan, allegiance is very much attached to one person, the driver behind the wheel. Every driver in that garage, however, has told me it is never simply about him or her. At this level of racing, it is very much about the talents and passion of those people around the driver. The best in the world will never win on talent alone. There are no lone rangers in racing, even though fans may see it that way from the stands.

How about you? Are you still trying to make it through life on your own, somehow secluded from others while you tend to your own crashes? Chances are there is more than just sheet metal damaged in your life; you may feel out of the race completely. Let me ask you to risk something. It may be frightening to you, but please give it a try. Look around you, right there in the community where you work and live. God desires to draw you into a place where you can heal and help heal others damaged in the wrecks of life. Most of the times we call a place like this "church."

Have you given up on church? Okay, let's not call it church. How about a faith community, fellowship, worship center, or gathering? What is it about those places that keep you from going back? Maybe it's because the people in there look like they have it all together and you know how far you are from that description. Maybe it is due to the shame you feel in having a self-inflicted wound. Let me close my thoughts with this encouragement to you. Churches are like pit stops in this way—full of people in as bad condition as you are, or worse, in need of fuel and restoration. A church service is not the race, it's the place you go to gain perspective on the race, how to run it, and to get the resources to do so. And when you find yourself in a crash, it's the place you go to find people who understand what it is like to suffer.

The people who make up this body exist on a human level to be an extension of God's grace to you by their acts and deeds. We gather regularly with others and meet headon the consistent barrage of life with the provisions of God. That is what church should be like anyway, a place to share with others in the presence of the Lord, a place where over time we find our broken hearts comforted and restored.

This is what I need from such a gathering, and I am guessing you do too. It is the place where I learn that in binding the hurts of others, I also find myself treated. To pretend that your heart is unbreakable will leave you bleeding in earnest and will encourage those around you to crank their self-made soul tourniquets even tighter. You don't have to live that way. All broken hearts hemorrhage, so where else can we go but to the Great Physician in the midst of his people to find repair? Like drivers who trust their pit crew, as believers we entrust ourselves to faith communities that help us heal. Life is full of bumps and crashes. If you haven't found this sort of authenticity in your place of worship, why don't you start it? Start slowly, but get going. You will be amazed at who comes off the track with you.

## PIT NOTE

God has not left you friendless. Right here in your community are authentic lovers of God and followers of Christ. You need them and they need you. Take a moment to think about who has been placed in your path for such a community. Ask God to lead you to a people who love him and others with all their hearts.

# part 5

## STAYING ON TRACK OFF THE TRACK

It is no secret that in the few moments between the rolls of their own thunder, there are even fewer moments when people in the racing world can reflect and relate. Yet those in this sport have a desire to explore the meaning of life just as much as you do. Maybe you grasp the idea that racers—yes, even the drivers—are people with the same challenges and opportunities you face. Or maybe you have fallen into the trap of thinking that your life pales in comparison with theirs, believing that fulfillment and success are always on their horizon and that they are exempt from the realities of your humdrum life.

All of us face the issues of character development that must be measured by the standard of our Creator. After all, we are created in God's image (Genesis 1:26-28). As you have seen so far, to follow Jesus and receive the Holy Spirit to guide you—that is to possess the resources for life change. There are no shortcuts or exemptions in character development. It comes when those who have journeyed further in their faith or life experience come together with those who are teachable. We have to make time, get off track if you will, if we want to stay on track in becoming like the Lord we follow.

# 21

## THE FINE ART OF WINNING AND LOSING

> In the same way, you younger men must accept
> the authority of the elders. And all of you, serve
> each other in humility, for "God opposes the
> proud but favors the humble." So humble your-
> selves under the mighty power of God, and at the
> right time he will lift you up in honor.
>
> 1 Peter 5:5-6

Dale Jarrett is proud of his kids. I met Dale in 1999 when
he was dominating the NASCAR Sprint Cup Series with
Robert Yates Racing. He even won the NASCAR Sprint
Cup Series championship that year. They were so blessed
by it all, and they made me feel like a part of the team. To
be there with that team after they had worked incessantly
year after year for a title was awe-inspiring. It's a year I will
never forget. My elation, however, could not compare
with the sheer ecstasy written on the faces of Dale, Kelley,
and their children.

Dale is pretty easy to talk with in general, but if you
really want to see him come alive, ask him about his kids.
They are a competitive threesome, two girls and a boy,
with a serious tenacity for sports. Each week I would
check in with Dale and ask, "So where are they this week-

end?" He would proceed to tell me what spot in the world Kelley had taken them; at the time it usually involved some Amateur Athletic Union (AAU) event. They understood why he could not accompany them, but that never seemed to make much of a difference to Dale. He wished he could be with them. But even racecar drivers can't be in two places at once.

Through the ministry of Motor Racing Outreach, and the work of Ron and Jackie Pegram in particular, Father's Day weekend is a time families usually come together, even if we were at the track. Ron and Jackie orchestrated "The Father's Day Olympics," where the sons and daughters of these heroes could compete alongside their dads. Many community members, including NASCAR officials, crew members, and media also turned out for this event. Dale and Zachary Jarrett, along with Ward and Jeb Burton, Jeff and Paige Burton, Bobby and Tyler Labonte, Dale and Taylor Earnhardt (to name a few) would take part in competitions that involved lots of mess and mayhem. When I tell people that I've raced against Bobby Labonte, they're less impressed when I inform them that it was relay race— on foot to a bowl of whipped cream, to find a gummy worm with no hands!

At one of these events, Zach was having an off day. Like most boys, he was facing a decision: either to give up or to continue and endure a poor showing. "Dad, I think I'll just quit," he told his champion father. "I'm not winning at anything." Dale pulled him aside and reminded him that he could not quit in life every time he did not cross the finish line first. "Imagine if I had quit every time I didn't finish first. We wouldn't be here today, would we? Now get back out there and do your best." Way to go, Dad!

The book of Proverbs is a collection of wisdom for us to live by. The writer of these sayings has made observations that God inspired him to pen. One of these observations, Proverbs 22:6 tells parents, "Train a child in the way he should go, and when he is old he will not turn from it." What Dale was leading Zach to that evening was one of many character-shaping moments that would affect the rest of his son's life. Nobody wins well who doesn't first learn how to lose well.

Our nature is not inclined to be humble. We must be taught. The humiliation that comes from being bested by our peers in sport is a somewhat sterile way for God to perform surgery on our ego. When you teach a child how to lose well, you form in her the ability to appreciate the victories with gratitude. Losing not only gives a young person an opportunity to improve in the activity, it plants the seeds of a grateful heart.

## PIT NOTE

Do you resist try something new because you're afraid you won't be good at it? If you're a parent, why not take some time this week to plan something that you can experience for the first time with your kids. As they see you responding well to the struggles of learning something new, you will give them courage to take important risks that will shape their lives. Let them know that you have to trust God in the big things and the small.

# 22

## WORTHY CAUSES

Then God said, "Let the earth produce every sort of animal, each producing offspring of the same kind—livestock, small animals that scurry along the ground, and wild animals." And that is what happened.... And God saw that it was good. Then God said, "Let us make human beings in our image, to be like us. They will reign over the fish in the sea, the birds in the sky, the livestock, all the wild animals on the earth, and the small animals that scurry along the ground."

Genesis 1:24-26

Now, a person who is put in charge as a manager must be faithful.

1 Corinthians 4:2

I continue to find Ward Burton remarkable. He was the first driver I met when I was interviewing with Motor Racing Outreach. We were in Bristol, Tennessee, and during a rain delay in practice, he and I ran into each other under the

MRO fitness tent. He was exercising and so was I, but he spoke to me first and we exchanged small talk. Thinking at the time he might be an MRO volunteer, I asked, "What do you do around here?" He gave me that classic chuckle under his breath, "Drive a race car, man." I was embarrassed. He loved it. We've been friends ever since.

For most of the racing seasons, my family traveled with me in a 35-foot motor home, bouncing from track to track. They did this because my wife worked in the children's ministry area. She would teach the kids in a Bible school atmosphere while their parents were trying to pass each other on the racetrack. The ability to travel with family increased my longevity with the ministry. On those occasions when we raced west of the Mississippi River, Ward was always gracious enough to let me fly with him. I enjoyed the drive from Charlotte, North Carolina, to his home near Danville, Virginia, where I would meet Ward and his pilot, Tommy Freeze. It was on those long flights from East Coast to West that I listened to Ward talk about his other passion—the land of his native state.

Virginia is one of those places so beautiful you want to carry a jar of the dirt with you on departure. Ward is as passionate about his homeland as anyone. I once saw him rise from a concussion injury, having said nothing up to that point, to correct a nurse who mistakenly told him that he would be back in North Carolina soon. Still in a neck brace and with his eyes closed, he yelled in her direction as she walked out the door, "*Virginia*!" It was all he had to say.

Ward told me that he started the Ward Burton Wildlife Foundation primarily because he felt compelled to be a good steward of creation. His particular spot in God's garden happens to be in Halifax County, but he doesn't stop there. Ward is on a mission to preserve as much natural habitat for posterity as possible. From his website at www.twbwf.org we read these words: "The mission of the Ward Burton Wildlife Foundation is to conserve America's land and wildlife through wise stewardship while educating children and adults about the natural resources that will shape America's future."

Like many of his fellow drivers who have a platform of influence, Ward believes that success in life is not measured by how many wins he collects on a racetrack, but by living responsibly with the gifts God has entrusted to him and by investing his life in service to others.

In Deuteronomy 8:17-18 we learn that God provides these gifts "so you would never say to yourself, 'I have achieved this wealth with my own strength and energy.' Remember the LORD your God. He is the one who gives you power to be successful, in order to fulfill the covenant he confirmed to your ancestors with an oath." God owns it all. We are called to manage his resources wisely.

Whether you are praying the most revered prayer in the Torah or heeding the words of Jesus, you are commissioned to love the Lord your God with all your heart, soul, mind, and strength—and to love your neighbor as yourself (see Deuteronomy 6:5; Leviticus 19:18; Matthew 22:36-40). Our causes should line up with what God values most—the glory of his character (Habakkuk 2:14). When we exercise our stewardship well, we discover the character and, indeed, the heart of our Creator.

## PIT NOTE

You don't have to be a NASCAR driver with lots of corporate backing and a foundation in your name to leave a legacy in this world. Take a minute and consider all that you possess. What circle of influence has God provided you? Do you have a young man or woman you are pouring your life into? What is your cause, and is it worthy of the Creator? Any cause we embrace has to be for the benefit of others as well as ourselves. Take Ward's example and embrace your own passion—and don't forget to bring others with you.

# 23

## PERFECT FOAM

God's will is for you to be holy, so stay away from
all sexual sin. Then each of you will control his
own body and live in holiness and honor—not in
lustful passion like the pagans who do not know
God and his ways.

1 Thessalonians 4:3-5, NLT

Don't you realize that your body is the temple of
the Holy Spirit, who lives in you and was given to
you by God? You do not belong to yourself, for
God bought you with a high price. So you must
honor God with your body.

1 Corinthians 6:19-20

Folks in NASCAR do not often use the phrase *at home*;
"in the shop" is more appropriate. When we are back in
Charlotte, however, I enjoy the time I get to spend with the
drivers and crews away from all the distractions of track
activity. In those moments we truly speak about life in a
deeper and more concentrated way. Coffee shops are a
great environment for these conversations.

When you meet a NASCAR driver in person, it can be a slightly intimidating thing. He may expect more admiration than you want to give, or he may not want any at all. A cup of coffee tends to put us on common ground. I love coffee, and a few drivers I know enjoy the stuff as well. Legend has it that this beverage charged the systems of Civil War soldiers with courage, so they drank as much as they could get their hands on. Perhaps racecar drivers drink it for the same reason—especially before qualifying!

Perhaps the aroma itself is enough to embolden some of us. Perhaps that is why, on one particular evening, I decided to go in a direction I had never gone before. You see, I'm from a place where coffee is simple. But my companion that evening challenged me to try a cappuccino.

I collected the fragrant brew, paid the perky college student behind the counter, and started to walk outside with my prize. Before I hit the door, the humble barista said, "Enjoy that work of art you're holding!" I was curious. "A work of art?" I repeated dubiously. "Sir, you are holding perfect foam," was the reply. Wow, I was holding perfect foam. So I pulled off the cap and sure enough there was foam. In fact, foam occupied about one-third of my cup. I was indignant with the celebrity next to me. "What have you talked me into here?" I just wanted coffee, and now some brew-snob behind the counter over there was cheating me out of liquid by what—trying to get me to value the foam? Foam as art? Perfect foam? What was that?

While I was protesting the ridiculousness of "perfect foam" masquerading as a cup of joe, my celebrity companion was distracted by the three young blondes who were checking him out. "Hey, pal," I prodded him. "Hate to spoil your moment of perceived *hotness*, but you stink at ordering coffee!" Still, I sat there and swallowed foam while I pondered the question for which this meeting was convened.

Bottom line—in less than a year, this young man had gone from a no-name kid who was inexperienced in love to a household name with more propositions than he could count. He was so overwhelmed that it isn't exaggerating to say he was frightened. That's right, a racecar driver in an off-track situation where he was scared. He bashfully asked me this incredibly honest question: "How can I take advantage of my new-found relational clout without it getting messy?" I inhaled and choked on foam.

"Let me see if I'm reading you right on this. By taking advantage, you mean: 'How can I sleep with these women and not break their hearts.' Right? You want to exercise your ego without guilt." I shook my head, "At least you are somewhat concerned about these women. That's something I guess. But it's not enough." He scowled, "Man, that's brutal." I sipped, "Yeah, but it's true, isn't it?"

You may envy his situation—young, famous, successful, and the object of others' desire. What more could a swinging single want—members of the opposite sex scrambling for attention and intimacy. This young man was perplexed, however, and for good reason. Had I been in his position at that age, I hope I would have handled it as well as he did—at least he sought my insight as a pastor and an older man. When he took a look at what it would feel like to enjoy a beautiful woman in a casually sexual way, he experienced tension. He wanted that pleasure—without damaging her soul. And deep down he knew it was not possible. To engage in such activity is to set a fire, a fire that starts out as passion but burns beyond the flesh and damages the soul. That was a price he was unwilling to pay. I hope he remains unwilling.

Without the foundation of commitment, casual—albeit passionate—sex becomes like the foam on my cappuccino. Foam is the empty, pretty stuff between the cap and coffee. Foam pleases my senses, but it does not quench my thirst. As we saw in the verses above, God places boundaries around the sexual component of who we are. We are created as sexual beings—that is not a bad thing. But as we looked at stewardship in the previous chapter, we see here that our bodies also remain under God's authority—even a *hot* racecar driver's body!

To be "bought with a high price" is to live within the bounds of God's will even regarding our sex drive. When it comes to sex, what God has created us to long for is beneath the foam, beneath the sex-act alone. My prayer is that when this particular driver is ready to meet commitment's challenge, I'll be blessed to get the call. I'll perform the wedding and go to the reception. We will sit down in celebration of that blessed union, and of course, I'll ask for coffee. Just coffee.

## PIT NOTE

Review the words of 1 Corinthians 6:19-20. Prayerfully consider what it means to you that the Lord has bought you with a price. Ask yourself what it would take for you to acknowledge God as the Lord in every area of your life. Not one of us has the strength to stay pure in this world in the way that God wants us to be. Take the time to identify those areas of your life where you struggle most with issues of purity, integrity, and godly character. Then ask God to fill you with Christ's own character, to live each day in complete dependence on the Spirit's strength, wisdom, and grace.

# 24

## KISS AND MAKE UP

Then Peter came to Jesus and asked, "Lord, how many times shall I forgive my brother when he sins against me? Up to seven times?" Jesus answered, "I tell you, not seven times, but seventy-seven times."

Matthew 18: 21-22

[Jesus said,] "God blesses those who work for peace, for they will be called the children of God."

Matthew 5:8

On October 3, 1999, we were in Martinsville, Virginia, for the final, physically grueling, short-track race of the season. At the end of the season, tempers flare more quickly and old scores get settled. After a few spins during this particular race, I started getting worried about two old friends who were dueling pretty hard out there. Tony Stewart and the late Kenny Irwin Jr. had competed against each other since they were teens. In the heat of the moment combined with the years of rivalry, a confrontation could not be avoided. The last spin put Tony in the wall and out of the car. His words and gestures to Kenny set the stage for a continued conflict. I wanted to do something—to be a peacemaker. My mentor in sports chaplaincy pulled me aside and told me to be patient. Then he relayed a story about another time and place, but a similar situation.

He told me of the time Darrell Waltrip was furious with Ricky Craven over an accident that Darrell held Ricky completely responsible for. During the next week's activities, Darrell and Ricky kept their distance from each other as Darrell stewed. The next race came and with it came the simmering tensions from the preceding day's events. However, one of those stops before the start of the race is always chapel service. Darrell was called upon to pray and read Scripture. He turned and faced the crowd, ready to read, but the look on DW's face, Max told me, was priceless. Darrell had locked eyes with Ricky Craven, who was also in the crowd. Darrell couldn't go on. In true DW fashion, he called Ricky forward and the two reconciled right there in front of God and everybody.* What a life lesson for the other drivers in attendance, as well as for the fans crowding alongside one another in that garage. That's the way you make peace with one another!

Restoring a relationship takes more time and courage than we normally want to invest. Personally, I would rather stand on my pride and wait for an apology than to extend my hand to reconciliation. We somehow think we deserve the other person's humble approach to our woundedness. In contrast, they deserve to grovel. It's here that I inevitably lock eyes with Jesus, and melt into a pool of confession—and gratitude that he doesn't demand my groveling. He doesn't insist that I wallow in shame. If you haven't grasped this already, I pray that you will now.

I want you to get it. I really want you to understand that while Jesus hung on the cross he absorbed the guilt, shame, and punishment that were meant to be owned by all of us. There really is nothing you can do to make God love you more than he already does. Any further demonstration would cheapen the message (see Romans 5:8; Galatians 4:4-7). It's from this state of peace that we can make amends with others (Matthew 6:12, 14). We can also create a space and atmosphere to allow people around us to reconcile with others, the way that Max's chapel service made possible a peace between Darrell and Ricky. He never actually brought the two of them together the way we might be tempted to think he should have. Max's story illustrated how God used him to create an environment for forgiveness.

I took his lesson to heart and left my friends to work out their differences with out my clumsy attempts to mediate. Two weeks after the race in Martinsville, we were back in Talladega for the final super-speedway race of the year. I walked into the drivers' meeting that morning and saw a sight that made me smile. Next to the wall stood one of those chest-high tables where inspectors could easily examine the parts they might place there. Those parts were long gone, fastened to the machines that awaited their respective asphalt pilots. But on the table, sitting close to one another and laughing boyish laughs were Tony Stewart and Kenny Irwin. Peace was also there. I'm glad it was. Kenny died less than a year later, at the age of 30. We never know when time might expire, and with it the opportunity to say "I'm sorry."

## PIT NOTE

Of all the men and women who have walked this earth, only Jesus has the right to hold a grudge. And yet, he doesn't. Even on the cross, Jesus spoke words of forgiveness for his executors and persecutors. And to this day, when you or I offend against God's love and God's law, we only need to confess our wrong and ask for pardon—and the Lord grants it willingly. Remember that grace, generous and undeserved, when you look in the face of someone who has wounded or offended you. Turn to God, the author of peace, and ask for the strength to forgive—and to seek forgiveness from an enemy—or friend.

* For more glimpses into the deeper side of DW, see *Darrell Waltrip: One on One* by Darrell Waltrip and Jay Carty (Ventura, CA: Regal Books, 2004).

# 25

## PASSING THE WHEEL

Timothy, my son, here are my instructions for you, based on the prophetic words spoken about you earlier. May they help you fight well in the Lord's battles. Cling to your faith in Christ, and keep your conscience clear. For some people have deliberately violated their consciences; as a result, their faith has been shipwrecked.

1 Timothy 1:18-19

For I am already being poured out like a drink offering, and the time has come for my departure. I have fought the good fight, I have finished the race, I have kept the faith. Now there is in store for me the crown of righteousness, which the Lord, the righteous Judge, will award to me on that day—and not only to me, but also to all who have longed for his appearing.

2 Timothy 4:6-8, NIV

On August 27, 2007, James Hylton turned 73 years old. That may not sound special to you, but combine it with the statistic that just six months earlier he became the oldest driver to attempt to qualify for the Daytona 500, it's downright remarkable. His story hit the sports world by storm, and it seemed every race fan in the country was pulling for him. James went on to run as high as second place in the Gatorade 150 qualifying race, until mechanical problems took him off the racetrack. Not bad for a guy who drove his first race in Manassas, Virginia, on July 8, 1964—three months before I was born.

Hylton's story reminded me that we not only pull for the underdogs of the world—we pull for the "old guys" as well. The year 2007 was a great year for the old guys on many levels. Three of my baseball-hurling heroes are still on the mound, digging deeper than ever. Greg Maddux, John Smoltz, and Tom Glavine, are all in their 40s and still getting it done. I remain inspired by Glavine's three-hundredth win—and counting. And what about football? Fifty-nine-year-old Mike Flynt returned to his West Texas alma mater, Sul Ross State and actually made the Division 3 college team. That's right. He walked on, tried out, and made the cut—a player eight years older than his coach! Go to any NASCAR Sprint Cup Series race in the near future, and you may still see Mark Martin, Rusty Wallace, or Bill Elliott climb behind the wheel. Ricky Rudd also came back in 2007 after a brief retirement. Rudd is the guy who actually taped one eye open to race in the Daytona 500. The year 2007 was the only year in Ricky's career where he couldn't make a start due to a physical injury.

The tenacity of true competitors and the drive to go head to head with others in sport is almost maddening at times. I have heard men and women speak of the angst that sitting in the stands causes them. The desire to "mix it up" in competition, to continue to leave a mark, appears never to expire in those who are dedicated to athleticism. I spoke with veteran driver Mark Martin while visiting the track: "Mark, I thought you retired! Now I guess I'll have to get back out here with you guys." "Naw," he said. "You've got all those boys at home. Stick to your guns." He sounded as if he was trying to convince himself as much as me.

In racing, the steering wheel is detachable. Attend any pre-race drivers' meeting and you will hear race director, David Hoots, remind the drivers to index their wheels. Not only does this give the proper alignment to the car's direction; it is a precautionary measure so the wheel is not removed from the column at race speed. But a detachable wheel also means it can be handed to another. That's a powerful metaphor in life and in ministry.

In the apostle Paul's two letters to a young pastor named Timothy, I sense that he is wrestling with a detachable wheel that he has held for quite some time. In another letter he speaks of this struggle more clearly by wishing on one hand to remain on earth and serve the purposes of spreading the gospel, but on the other hand to depart to be with the Lord (Philippians 1:22-24). Paul talks like an old man still driven to war for the kingdom of God, but prepared to present his sword to a younger generation of Christ-followers he has helped establish. Was he ever fully prepared to step aside? I wonder.

As we grow older in this walk of faith, my prayer for us is that we will always live with an eye on departure. Doing so, I think we can keep our roles through the seasons of our lives in check. If we get to the place where we still want to "race" based on the desire for more heroics or control, we are not serving the Lord's agenda. If our identity is wrapped up in the particular role we play in life, we forfeit the chance to give the wheel to another. I confess my own struggle with this thought, no matter how far in the future it may be.

Even Jesus himself said that it was to the benefit of spreading the gospel that he return to his Father (John 14:12; Acts 1:6-11). He was willing to pass the wheel to his followers, and as a result the gospel is still reaching the remotest parts of the earth. It should continue to drive our courage that this news of salvation through Jesus Christ started with twelve unlikely individuals. We celebrate these heroes and others like them, but do we think it possible to achieve more than admiration from the sidelines? I think so.

If we grow old and miss the opportunities to outlive ourselves with trusted Timothys, I think we have failed no matter the tally of personal victories. Yes, we run the race on our own, but we must pass along what we know. That is why I wrote this book. Until now, I didn't really think I had much to say. I am just now coming to terms with the influence Christ has entrusted to me—and my responsibility (and privilege) to expand it.

There is a finish line for each of us. I believe, like Paul, that if we live long enough to see those we have trained surpass our accomplishments, we excel with them. I must be willing to pass the wheel, however, so others may run farther.

## PIT NOTE

No one lives forever. Ask God to place men and women in your life who will take what God has entrusted to you and go further than you have gone. Never see your life in only a temporary light, but pray that God's purposes will be established in and through you, so that the Lord's influence will go forward until the day of his glorious return.

# epilogue

## GETTING TO VICTORY LANE

The day is coming when your pride will be brought low and the LORD alone will be exalted.

Isaiah 2:11

For the time will come when all the earth will be filled, as the waters fill the sea, with an awareness of the glory of the LORD.

Habakkuk 2:14

Don't hide your light under a basket! Instead, put it on a stand and let it shine for all. In the same way, let your good deeds shine out for all to see, so that everyone will praise your heavenly Father.

Matthew 5:15-16

I have always felt out of place showing up in Victory Lane. Prior to 2001 tradition was that the chaplain greeted the winner and maybe even prayed with him before he left the car for an interview and celebration. Earnhardt would often pull me into the #3 and give me a headlock to express his joy. First-time winners were often shocked to see me there: "Hey! You're the last guy I saw before I hit the ignition and the first guy I saw when I killed the motor. Cool!"

I understood that my role there was not to try to be a member of the team. I wasn't there to be accepted into the partylike atmosphere, even though I usually was. My role was to be a reminder for them to put God first and thank him for the victory. I functioned like a walking steeple, pointing in another direction. But things changed after the 2000 season. It was, after all, a new millennium.

Two of my good friends in the sport had the difficult task of asking me to stay out of the postrace event. I hope they saw my response as almost a relief instead of a disappointment. You have to understand that Victory Lane was full of people—many who belonged there even less than I did—and the TV producers were becoming more and more hindered in doing their jobs. With my already marginal enthusiasm about being there, I fully understood the move to "clean up Victory Lane."

In doing so, however, something my predecessor said to me became prophetic: "Beav', this sport is a world of extreme highs and lows. You will be most effective if you are visible and available during those times. There is no greater high for these guys on a weekly basis than when they're in Victory Lane. You forge relationships during those moments and gain greater influence as well." After I stopped going to the postrace production, I saw—as did millions of race fans—the fulfillment of this prophecy.

"Hey, Preacher, how come we don't hear the drivers thanking the Lord anymore? Why don't they thank God after the race like they used to?" I have heard this question all over the country, and while I do not believe the chaplain's absence in Victory Lane has everything to do with it, the void of a pastoral presence and reminder there is obvious. In a world of self-absorbed celebrities and heroes, we long for flickers of humility and gratitude. In the world of sports, we long for those who seem so much better than we are to acknowledge one better and greater than they are. Victory Lane was the platform for such a confession, and the chaplain was there to remind the victorious of the greater reality.

In his book *The Gospel According to Starbucks*, Leonard Sweet describes the concept of cultural celebrity worship in terms I have been wrestling with for a few years now. He writes,

> We idolize what we admire. Writers idolize writers. Athletes idolize athletes. Maybe Christians need to help idols de-idolize their lives and become icons. That is the way we can play the celebrity card without falling into the celebrity trap....You pray to an idol....You pray through an icon. An icon is a window through which you look to God....Our hope is not in idols. Our hope is in God.

Sweet nails the point home for us with this closing remark: "Icons, by inviting us to look through them to God, make us more wise and good and holy, and more dependent on God."* I do not watch televised races much anymore, I think in part because I don't have the perspective of glorifying God to look forward to.

We all deal with the need for approval and acceptance, even hunger for it at times. You don't have to own a souvenir business built on your image and autograph to realize that you want to feel special. Yet when we demand glory from others that rightfully belongs to Christ, we are heading for destruction. What I have found among celebrities (idols) who fully absorb the praise of their fan base is a loss of touch with themselves and reality. Praise from others that is not deflected to the Creator of all things becomes poison in the life of one who accepts it. Frankly, in seeking to possess so much, the idol goes on to lose his or her mind! Need I cite the tabloids?

I reserve this final entry to remind you to be careful not only *where* you place your affections and to *whom*, but also to remind you that we really do live as one of the great confessions of faith says, "to glorify God and enjoy him forever." Life is not about us. The apostle is clear; our bodies are the temple of the Holy Spirit (1 Corinthians 3:16). It is not the temple that receives worship but that which inhabits it. Ascribe your worship and the worship of others to the one who truly deserves it. Such is required of the victorious life.

## PIT NOTE

Where do you spend most of your time and money? To whom do you give your allegiance? Don't answer too quickly. In the absence of another, you may have placed yourself on the throne. Let Christ have the seat.

* Leonard Sweet, *The Gospel According to Starbucks* (Colorado Springs: Waterbrook Press, 2007).

# appendix

## EULOGY FOR DALE EARNHARDT SR.

**NOTE:** *This eulogy was delivered by the author on Thursday, February 22, 2001, at Calvary Chapel, Charlotte, North Carolina, for the Celebration of Life memorial service broadcast live across the nation.*

I don't know about you but over the last couple days I've been searching for a place to anchor my hope. When times like this come—and they come for all of us—we look for a place to anchor for stability. Today we want to celebrate and remember the life and person who was Dale Earnhardt.

I want to encourage you to do three things in the coming days. To tell those stories—and everybody sitting here has a Dale Earnhardt story—and remember the emotion that goes with those stories. To listen to each other as you tell those stories. And to pray. Pray alone and with one another. I think Dale would be happy that we will be laughing and telling stories with each other.

Where do we go from here? I mean, all of us, we don't like thinking about the death of a loved one—or about our own death for that matter. How do we find comfort? How do we anchor to something?

My friend Dave Haney says it better than I could. He writes in his book *A Living Hope*:

> ...to imagine that there's no such thing as absolute truth is essentially a corruption of the hope that we have in Christ. When Jesus said in John 14:6 that he is the Way, the Truth and the Life he gave a fairly strong indication to us that there are absolutes in the world, and that he is the standard of those absolutes. No wonder we as people of faith suffer from the symptoms of chronic loss of hope.*

This happens due to bombardment of our current culture which holds to no standard for truth. If we fall prey to this assault, Dave goes on to say that we might just as well anchor our hope into "warm Jell-O."

I hope that you will find that you can anchor into a deeper hope as you look into this text that Pastor John Cozart has read today and as we reflect on this passage (John 11:1-45).

I want you to think for just a moment about the first time you met Dale Earnhardt. Remember the first time you met Dale? I remember the first time I met Dale. I have the opportunity to be a chaplain with the Motor Racing Outreach, and I go from track to track. I'm kind of a pastor and a chaplain who visits with the men who not only own and work on these teams but who drive these race cars as well. I remember that I was very young in this ministry—about six months going along.

And Lonnie Clouse, who was our youth pastor, wanted to take some of the kids on a camping trip in Pocono. And we were at this beautiful place, and we were going to take the kids to the Pocono Mountains. Taylor [Earnhardt] wanted to go on this camping trip, or I think she did anyway. And Lonnie came to me and said, "Yo, dude, I need you to take this permission slip to Big E and get him to sign it, because [Taylor] wants to go on this camping trip." And I said, "Okay, I'll do it. I'll be glad to do that."

As I started walking toward the garage, I knew that meant that I was going to have to be in the presence of Dale for the first time. And so I thought to myself, *I've developed a pretty good relationship with Richard Childress's PR guy, J.R., so I'll do an end-run around this and give the permission slip to J.R. and have him take it to Dale. It'll all be handled. I'll get the permission slip, and we can go on our way.* So I gave it to J.R.

Twenty minutes later I came back, and J.R. was looking at me with the permission slip in his hand, and it didn't have the signature on it. J.R. said, "He wants to see you a few minutes." And I said, "He wants to see me? J.R., would you take me to him?"

"Yeah, yeah, c'mon."

We got up on the transporter and walked these few feet to the back cubby hole that's a lounge, and we are walking down what seemed like miles into this dark place in the back. I said, "What kind of a mood…what's he doing?" And J.R. said, "He's having lunch."

I said, "Oh great, he's killed a bear there this morning, and he's sitting in the back of this thing eating a bear with his bare hands, and I'm gonna be dessert because I want to take his daughter on a camping trip." So as we got to the back and J.R. introduced me, I didn't find a man eating a bear. I didn't see deer heads on the walls. I saw a man eating an orange.

I saw a man eating an orange, who with a very warm demeanor welcomed me into his presence. I didn't come into the presence of a racing icon or an intimidating figure. I came into the presence of a dad who was concerned about his daughter. And I know he was concerned about all his children and grandchildren.

He asked me for the next few moments what our intentions were, with Taylor going on this camping trip. When would we be back? It's interesting, because I walked out of there getting a lesson in parenthood. I told Dale, "Dale, if you're concerned about this, I certainly understand, because I have two boys, and I don't want them to cross the street." I connected with him there. He said, "Yeah, yeah. That's right." He said, "They grow up fast, and you need to spend as much time with them as you can." I walked away from there that day welcomed into the presence of a father.

And that's what I want you to think about today. Because ultimately, that's on a physical level what we can relate to on a spiritual level. The Scripture that Pastor Cozart just read talks about Jesus coming into a situation with a family he loved. These were not just casual acquaintances who were in need. These were people with whom Jesus was intimately involved. He was their friend. And Jesus came into this situation emotionally, and he was looking at the disciples and saying that Lazarus was dead. In fact, he said, "I'm glad I wasn't there." And I'm thinking, *Wait just a minute.*

If Jesus could have been there, he would have healed him and he would not have died. Why would Jesus be excited that his friend Lazarus was gone? I stand by the cars of all you guys, as I have stood by the car with Dale and Teresa before. And we always ask, "God protect these men as they get into their race cars. Protect these teams in their own pit row, please. And don't let anything happen to them today. Give them a safe race." And most of the time God grants that request and we rejoice as we go home.

But sometimes he doesn't. And Jesus would look at us and say, "I'm glad I wasn't there." Why in the world would he choose to miss intervening in these situations in our lives? He did it for the disciples, I think, for the same reason he does it for us today—so that we will see and experience his greater glory. Do you catch that? Jesus moves through the passage as he meets and greets Martha and her sister who are grieving over the situation. He helps them answer the question of life that every one of us sitting here today is asking. And the question you and I are asking is whether death is the most powerful force in the universe. I could tell you, as we read from the beginning, that if death is the most powerful force in the universe and there are no absolutes for you and me to anchor our faith in, then we are in trouble. We are in deathly grave trouble.

But Jesus came along and said to the sister, "I am the resurrection and the life. Anyone who believes in me even though they die yet shall they live." Do you hear those words? Will you let that sink in today? Because if that is an absolute truth that standards flow from, then you and I have a hope that is more sustaining than warm Jell-O. We have the bedrock of life for today and forevermore. That's what I want you to see today. Interesting, isn't it?

Martha says, "Yes, Lord, I know that my brother will rise at the resurrection at the last day." But Jesus is taking her to a more immediate act of faith. He says, "I am the resurrection and the life. He who believes in me, even though he is dead, yet shall he live."

Later on in the passage, in verse 40, we have these words: " 'Didn't I tell you that you would see God's glory if you believe?' So they rolled the stone aside and Jesus looked up to heaven and said, 'Father, thank you for hearing me. You always hear me, but I said it out loud for the sake of all these people standing here so they would believe that you sent me.'" Notice that? Then Jesus shouted, "Lazarus, come out!" And Lazarus came out, bound in grave clothes, his face wrapped in a head cloth. And Jesus told the people around him, because Lazarus was wrapped in grave clothes, to unwrap him and let him go. Verse 45 says that many of the people who were with Mary believed in Jesus when they saw this happen.

Would you believe in absolutes with me today? Because the absolute truth is that Christ has provided a way for all of us. When I walked that day into the presence of greatness—I don't have to tell you that Dale Earnhardt was great—I went with a person and found a father. See the connection here?

I don't want to liken J.R. to Jesus too much here! I'm not out to try and compare you with him, buddy. I'm not up here to say that Dale Earnhardt was God. That's not it at all. But I'm saying that you and I will one day be ushered into the presence of a very intimidating force. And we have the privilege based on this passage today to have somebody do it with us. Jesus says I'll take you there. Jesus is not just a public relations manager. He is the Savior of the world, and he can escort you into the presence of greatness to where you will feel no fear and you will find rest for your soul and the presence of a Dad. That's what you can trust. That's where you can hope. There is a Savior who will take you there. I wonder if you know him?

Father God, thank you so very much for the mediation of your Word and the hope that we find in you. Thank you so very much for loving this family and for the way I have seen you move in their midst over the last couple of days. What a precious privilege it is to sit here in a house of worship and remember your goodness to a man we love. And we thank you because we know that our hope does not lie in something that is empty, but in something that can save our souls. Be with us on this day for Christ's sake. Amen.

* From the Introduction of David Haney's *A Living Hope: The Comfort and Assurance That Comes from Knowing God Cares for You* (Wheaton: Crossway Books, 1999).

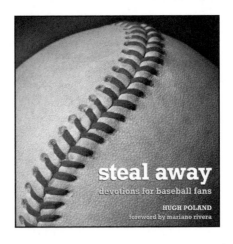

*A grand slam devotional
for the spirit and soul
of baseball fans!*

## STEAL AWAY: Devotions
## for Baseball Fans

### Hugh Poland; Foreword by Mariano Rivera

"*I sense in* Steal Away *a familiar passion both for baseball
and for following Christ.*"

—Mariano Rivera, New York Yankees

"*From the locker room to the upper room, the Scriptures
come to life through America's greatest pastime! This
book should be a part of every sports fan's collection.*"

—Jeff Hutcheon, Fellowship of Christian Athletes

"*You will be spiritually challenged, greatly encouraged,
and wonderfully entertained.*"

—Kent Bottenfield, former Major League pitcher

"Steal Away *combines Scripture with many interesting stories from the rich history of baseball to provide a collection of wonderful devotionals that anyone who loves the game of baseball will find uplifting.*"

—Vince Nauss, President, Baseball Chapel

"*...Poland weaves together a winning combination of great baseball quotes with various impacting passages of Scripture.*"

—CBN.com - The Christian Broadcasting Network

"*...a unique and remarkable collection of baseball feats and facts with a deftly intertwined understanding of Jesus and the scriptures...Thoughtful and thought-provoking, Steal Away is very highly recommended reading for all Christian baseball fans.*"

—*Midwest Book Review*

With grace and passion, Hugh Poland shines light on the real soul of baseball by providing testimonies of its soldiers of the game. Drawing upon stories from current and former players and managers, including the famous and the unsung heroes, the author shares life's important lessons through the lens of baseball's most memorable people and events.    978-0-8170-1491-9 $13.00

To order, call Judson Press at 800-4-JUDSON,
or visit www.judsonpress.com.
Save 20% when you order online!

JUDSON PRESS
PUBLISHERS SINCE 1824